MW00584248

The Rule of the Rich?

*Adam Smith's Argument
Against Political Power*

SUSAN E. GALLAGHER

The Rule of the Rich?

The Pennsylvania State University Press
University Park, Pennsylvania

Library of Congress Cataloging-in-Publication Data

Gallagher, Susan E.
　　The rule of the rich? : Adam Smith's argument against political
power / Susan E. Gallagher.
　　　　p.　cm.
　　Includes bibliographical references and index.
　　ISBN 0-271-01774-0 (cloth : alk. paper)
　　　　1. Smith, Adam, 1723–1790—Contributions in political science.
I. Title.
JC176.S63G35　1998
320'.01'1—dc21　　　　　　　　　　　　　　　　　　　　98-20730
　　　　　　　　　　　　　　　　　　　　　　　　　　　　　　CIP

Copyright © 1998 The Pennsylvania State University
All rights reserved
Printed in the United States of America
Published by The Pennsylvania State University Press,
University Park, PA 16802-1003

It is the policy of The Pennsylvania State University Press to use acid-free paper for
the first printing of all clothbound books. Publications on uncoated stock satisfy the
minimum requirements of American National Standard for Information Sciences—
Permanence of Paper for Printed Library Materials, ANSI Z39.48-1992.

CONTENTS

ACKNOWLEDGMENTS

In its evolution from undergraduate paper to Ph.D. dissertation to first book, this project has, I am happy to say, gradually assumed much smaller proportions. For this and other fortunate developments, I am grateful to many mentors, colleagues, friends, and family members. These include the members of my dissertation committee, Ira Katznelson, Robert L. Heilbroner, Jacob Landynski, and George Shulman. I also received helpful advice on various drafts from Laurence Dickey, Gordon Schochet, and Isaac Kramnick.

For more general encouragement, support, and inspiration, I am thankful to Laura Barney, Anne K. Gallagher, Ellen M. Gallagher, Martha M. Gallagher, Andrew Hemingway, Alice O'Connor, Harold Katz, Lori Medici Fleming, and Yvonne Swann. Finally, I am happy to have an opportunity to express my gratitude to Carol Duncan for the guidance, reassurance, and friendship she has given me over the years. When I arrived at Ramapo College in 1979, Carol not only gently let me know about the gaps in my self-education, she introduced me to the profound pleasures of studying politics, culture, and history. Today, in my teaching, I do my best to follow her example by never underestimating how much my students can accomplish when they are given a fair opportunity. Meanwhile, in my scholarship, I do not pretend to match Carol's brilliance, but I follow her lead by keeping in mind that academics are usually most effective when we do not take ourselves too seriously.

Introduction

O f the many things Mandeville, Bolingbroke, Hume, and Smith have in common, perhaps the most decisive is that all four lived in an aristocratic society, that is, a society shaped by the notion that the propertied minority ought to be morally superior to the *mobile vulgus*, the vacillating crowd. Within this bygone context, the rich were not only supposed to use their leisure to develop a higher degree of humanity; they were also expected to exercise their excellence by watching over the moral and material welfare of their inferiors, that is, everyone else.

Today, of course, property ownership no longer entails such patriarchal duties. Increasing inequality in post-industrial societies, especially in the United States, has lately led many theorists to reflect anew about the gulf between haves and have-nots.[1] The aristocratic notion that the rich ought to care for the poor has, however, generally been forsaken not because it contravenes democracy, unfortunately, but because any program built on that conviction would simply cost too much. On a more historical level, we may identify what is no longer current about aristocratic assumptions about social inequality by recollecting that the same logic that tied the possession of property to moral identity implied that property owners who fulfilled their obligations truly deserved obedience, deference, and respect. From this standpoint, the rich were genuinely perceived to be different not, as Hemingway remarked, because they had more money or, as a present-day American might guess, because they hit the right numbers in the state lottery or, as a couple of gadflies have recently suggested, because they picked the right answers on an I.Q. test,[2] but because they were destined to "govern, guide, and represent their country" and therefore comprised the head of the social body, the thinking portion of the otherwise oblivious social whole.[3]

Although we have scant record of what the majority in eighteenth-century British society thought of this arrangement, we do know that they were expected not merely to submit to the laws of property, but to revere the rich as persons and, as required, step aside, lower their eyes, curtsy, bow, or touch their caps. The rich, as talk shows and tabloids currently attest, still elicit enormous attention, and some receive amazing amounts of concern and adulation. Nevertheless, just as the public no longer expects them to fulfill any definite civic purpose, they almost never insist on popular obeisance. The more fortunate may, in other words, continue to command the envy and admiration of the less fortunate— who would surely like to have similar access to body guards, credit cards, health spas, housing, food, education, and whatever else might be included among the finer things in life—but the level of popular servility aristocrats once exacted belongs to a world that even the most nostalgic scholars must describe as "lost."[4]

While disputes over how this loss occurred continue, historians of eighteenth-century British culture and society have lately been inclined to agree that the ruling elite stepped away from many of the moral ideals commonly attached to aristocracy—such as benevolence, largess, and compassion—long before they suffered any reduction of pre-eminence, wealth, or power. This growing consensus is particularly evident in the similarities between the findings of historians who study the eighteenth century from above, focusing mainly on the aristocracy, and those of historians who study it from below, focusing mainly on the "plebs" or the crowd.

In the first case, whatever disagreements may remain about the fate of lesser gentry, recent scholarship on the landed elite has rejected long-standing assumptions about decline in order to emphasize how well aristocrats responded to commercial progress. Thanks to enclosures and other agricultural innovations, increasing participation in government service and the professions, marriages arranged to infuse old estates with newly-made fortunes, and feverish competition for titles, honors, and pensions, the aristocracy emerged at the end of the century richer, more imperious, and more politically potent than it had ever been before.[5] Scholarship on popular culture confirms these conclusions. These studies point out that agricultural improvements portioned off the commons, the growing prominence of landowners in politics and the professions translated into a stream of property-protecting legislation, and the unprecedented prosperity of the uppermost members of the commercial aristocracy made them increasingly unaccountable, not only because their wigs and costumes were specifically designed to make them seem inaccessible, but because they lived in ever more imposing mansions and insulated parks, protected by bailiffs, snares, gardens, gates, and walls.[6]

Whether this set of social developments is characterized as a process of economic rationalization or as a slide into moral degradation, its upshot is that market relations prevailed over "vestigial moral preferences,"[7] and Britain became, in Adam Smith's words, "what is properly a commercial society" long before the end of aristocracy was anywhere in sight.[8] While this polarized picture has been criticized because it seems to deny the existence of the middling orders, most historians, including those who chronicle eighteenth-century middle-class advancement, tend to emphasize that aristocratic ascendancy remained largely unchallenged until 1832, when, in the face of heroic orations on the beauties of Old Corruption, the Reform Act passed.[9] Thus, whatever correlations poets might draw between "kind hearts and coronets," the decidedly unpaternalistic economic and political practices of those who prospered most in this period give us good reason to describe eighteenth-century Britain as a highly competitive, market-based society, while at the same time, the increasing concentration of wealth and political influence in the hands of the nobility gives us no reason to doubt the strength of aristocratic rule.

Though I have tried to approach this set of social relations with a maximum degree of historical specificity, there is no denying that eighteenth-century discussions of the relationship between wealth and poverty sometimes sound remarkably like present-day reflections on what can or cannot be done about increasing inequality. In 1795, for example, Edmund Burke advised the British elite to quit complaining about the condition of the laboring poor: "Let there be no lamentation," he insisted, "of their condition. It is no relief to their miserable circumstances; it is only an insult to their miserable understandings. . . . Want of one kind was never relieved by want of any other kind. Patience, labour, sobriety, frugality, and religion should be recommended to them; all the rest is downright *fraud*."[10] In 1995, outlining steps that might be taken to free both British and American society from the apparently unbearable weight of the welfare state, Gertrude Himmelfarb recommended that the underclass be instructed to embrace a similar set of virtues, including, in addition to "cleanliness and thrift," "family, fidelity, chastity, sobriety," and "personal responsibility."[11]

The similitude among such statements might inspire generalizations about how much easier it is to spell out why some people deserve next to nothing than it is to explain why others merit more than most people can imagine. However, as tempting as it is to emphasize the resemblance between late eighteenth- and late twentieth-century solutions to rising inequality, there is, as the following chapters are designed to show, a world of difference between the moral and political questions raised by the emergence of commercial modernity and the problems entailed in what some people see as its end.

In order to grasp the first set of questions, I have tried to explicate the strains commercial progress placed on the moral authority of the British aristocracy and determine how those tensions informed philosophical views of the relationship between property and power. In respect to the second set of problems, I can only make the obvious observation that we seem to be experiencing an especially excruciating period in the pained relationship between democracy and capitalism, and while that circumstance pervades the perspective taken here, it falls beyond the philosophies explored in this book. I shall, therefore, relegate the parallels between late eighteenth-century and late twentieth-century approaches to social disparity to a brief postscript. If, in the meantime, any readers wonder what sort of justification I might have for regarding the texts here considered as antiquated relics, the best answer I can offer is that this is a study of history rather than a study of "great books," "fundamental truths," or "perennial wisdom." I have, consequently, searched these works not for answers to inveterate questions, but for signs of significant social change.[12]

1

Commerce and the Question,
Who Should Rule?

uring the first half of the eighteenth century, a battery of civic-minded poets, playwrights, philosophers, and pamphleteers proclaimed that the commercial policies and practices of the Whig oligarchy were so corrupting British society that the natural rulers of the nation, the gentry and the nobility, were losing their capacity to discern and defend the interests of their country. During the second half of the eighteenth century, as it became increasingly clear that the commercial pursuits of the British aristocracy enhanced rather than harmed national prosperity, Adam Smith developed a far-reaching theory of historical evolution based on the proposition that purely self-regarding individuals promote social ends that extend far beyond their own narrow comprehension. These two phenomena are, I shall argue, so intimately interrelated that they may be described as cause and effect. To summarize this study in a single sentence: Smith's insight into the unintended benefits of economic competition developed in response to the seemingly depraved proclivities of the propertied elite in eighteenth-century Britain.[1]

While identifying Smith as a critic of aristocracy may sound like a shibboleth from the nineteenth century, I must emphasize that, as obvious as this thesis is, it is not a case of what has been described as "déjà vu all over again." Rather, by explicating Smith's adverse reaction to Whig oligarchy, I hope to overturn the relatively recent idea that Scottish political economy evolved as a vindication of the commercial Whig regime. In order to explain how Smith, the original "mouthpiece of bourgeois ideology," came to be implicated in a defense of aristocracy, it is necessary to recapitulate an approach that has been known as the "revisionist" reading of political discourse in early modern Britain, but that may now be designated as the prevailing paradigm in the study of eighteenth-century British political thought.[2]

Thanks to three decades of historical investigation, the long-lived vision of eighteenth-century Britain as the scene of a world-historical struggle between a rising middle class and a declining aristocracy has generally given way to the realization that, rather than being elbowed off the historical stage, the nobility and, to a lesser extent, the gentry solidified their supremacy by taking full advantage of the novel opportunities created by the commercialization of agriculture, the rise of the stock market, and the use of public funds to finance the national debt.[3] This post-Marxist approach, which underscores both the flexibility and the stability of aristocratic ascendancy, has been employed by J. G. A. Pocock and others to open a new line of inquiry into the making of commercial modernity.[4] More specifically, having accepted the aristocracy as full participants in commercial progress, students of British politics, literature, painting, and other subjects have been trying to explicate the ideological consequences of the commercialization of aristocratic property and its concomitant, political power.[5]

Though no historian has campaigned as strenuously as Pocock has to banish the word "bourgeois" from discussions of eighteenth-century Britain, most have jettisoned that term in order to advance the notion that the central ideological conflict of the period unfolded within the aristocracy.[6] In the "paper war" waged between supporters of the "Court," or ruling-Whig regime, and their opponents, a collection of Old Whigs and Tories who claimed to uphold the standards of the "Country," a generation of historians has discovered a class divided against itself.

On one side, the Court Whigs, exemplified, above all, by Robert Walpole, Britain's first prime minister, stood for modernity, stability, and commercial expansion.[7] On the other, the Country party, led by the "anti-minister," Henry St. John, Viscount Bolingbroke, championed the classical republican vision of the autonomous, virtuous, land-owning citizen in order to counter the apparently corrupt tendencies within the new commercial age.[8] The characterization of British political discourse in the early eighteenth century as a contest between Court Whig patrons of commercial progress and Country proponents of republican reform immediately invited a review of later developments.[9] Consequently, in keeping with the tendency of the republican paradigm to swallow everything in its path, various historians, notably Nicholas Phillipson, John Robertson, Donald Winch, and Christopher Berry, as well as Pocock, have argued that Scottish political economy, represented mainly by the writings of David Hume and Adam Smith, emerged as an answer to the Country party's case against the modern Whig ascendancy.[10]

Along these lines, Hume has been cast as the philosopher of refinement, an historically informed and sociologically oriented theorist who rejected the uncivilized austerity of classical republicanism in favor of the polished manners, humane pleasures, and bounteous prosperity generated by commercial interdependence and exchange. Although, as far as I know, only one historian, John Robertson, has gone so far as to claim that Hume beheld the material preconditions for universal citizenship in commercial development, it seems to be widely accepted that Hume overcame the moral expectations of the republican tradition by reducing the Country party's program for political reformation to an unnatural, insupportable, and generally hypocritical campaign against polite conversation, cultivated taste, and innocent ease.[11]

Smith, Hume's close friend, has likewise been positioned in relation to the civic tradition as a "realistic" respondent to the excessive austerity of classical republican thought. Portrayed, on one hand, as a civic-minded professor of provincial morality and, on the other, as a cosmopolitan contributor to the "science of the legislator," Smith has been drawn as a defender of commercial improvement against the antiquated requirements of republican rectitude.[12] For the republican principles of autonomy, dispassion, and disciplined dedication to the public good, Smith, it has been argued, substituted an Addisonian appreciation for the socially, culturally, and politically edifying features of commercial intercourse. Although, as far as I know, only Robertson has gone so far as to claim that Smith affirmed the republican concept of participatory liberty by extending it to include the laborers who, as Smith observed, actually produce national prosperity, there seems to be some agreement that the "civic dimension" or "civic flavor" of his writings stemmed from an effort to alter or negotiate the demands of civic humanism in order to find a place for politics in modern commercial life.[13] Smith's political program, from this perspective, could be defined as an attempt to explain how improving aristocrats might be counted as competent citizens, an explanation which would indicate that commercial aristocracy, contrary to the assertions of the Country party, should not be rejected as a contradiction in terms.[14]

My argument with these interpretations is not that any have overrated the insights to be gleaned from locating Scottish political economy within the ideological context created by the conflict between Court and Country. Instead, in my view, these accounts come to confused conclusions about eighteenth-century political philosophy because they begin with an incomplete recognition of the moral problems raised by commercial change. Specifically, what is missing from these studies is an adequate appreciation of the way republican terms were used in the eighteenth century, not only to criticize commerce as anathema to virtue, but, more comprehensively, as a means to preserve a moral basis for aristocratic rule.

When Bolingbroke and his compatriots castigated Walpole for placing private gain above public duty, they spoke, as Hume put it, "in the republican stile," because the republican link between property ownership and political capacity supplied a coherent moral framework for social, economic, and political inequality.[15] The Country party accordingly warned the political elite away from stock speculation, political patronage, and investments in public credit with the admonition that these activities would rob aristocrats of their moral identity by transforming property from an anchor of political integrity into an object of limitless desire. This utterly corrupting transformation would, the Country writers cautioned, turn the world upside down, converting wealth into destitution, reducing patricians to prostitution, and elevating those who least deserved to rule to the head of government.

Rather than directly contradicting previous accounts of Country ideology, this approach identifies aristocratic anxiety about the strength of social hierarchy as the heart and soul of the republican critique of commercial progress. From this standpoint, the central issue raised in the clash between Court and Country and explored in Hume and Smith's accounts of commercial society, was whether property could be or should be interpreted as an indication of civic capacity and, therefore, upheld as a platform for aristocratic supremacy. In short, the cardinal question asked in Country ideology and answered in Scottish social theory was whether the pandemic drive to get and spend severed the moral connections between aristocratic property, probity, and power.

OUTLINE OF CHAPTERS

In order to describe the moral uncertainty induced by the commercial revolution, I begin with Mandeville's deflationary celebration of the pursuit of private gain. Starting with Mandeville's work is somewhat problematic because his unflagging effort to expose the hypocrisy inherent in every conviction tends to make every objection to his thesis feel like a blast of hot air. However, contrasting Mandeville's parody of aristocratic pretension with Bolingbroke's dread of upper-class corruption helps to illuminate exactly what made the paradox presented in the *Fable of the Bees* both controversial and entertaining. By depicting private vices as public benefits, Mandeville defined the degradation of the elite as the surest source of general plenty. Mandeville's grandest joke and Bolingbroke's greatest fear were, in this respect, precisely the same: both insisted that modern modes of getting and spending reduced the distinctions of rank, education, and fortune to empty illusions—a reduction that, to Mandeville's delight and Bolingbroke's horror, overcame every moral difference between the rulers and the ruled.

Country writers, including Bolingbroke, Henry Fielding, Alexander Pope, Jonathan Swift, and John Gay, countered Mandeville's paradox by preaching up the notion that elites must lead by moral example to prevent the poor from sliding into idleness, luxury, and crime.[16] More consistently than his contemporaries, however, Bolingbroke emphasized the economic activities of the Whig supremacy as a threat to the civic integrity of the aristocracy and, consequently, as an invitation to political decline. The primary accusation Bolingbroke hurled at Walpole and his party was that by substituting devotion to private interest for dedication to public duty, the Whig oligarchy undermined the patriotic purpose of property, turning it from a support for political authority into a fountain of turpitude.

Hume rejected Bolingbroke's prognosis not because it was morally wrong, but because it was historically inaccurate and politically incorrect. Like Bolingbroke, Hume regarded the pursuit of private advantage as a threat to political capacity and as a danger to national integrity. But in contrast to Bolingbroke's republican obsession with civic virtue, Hume identified custom, habit, and tradition as the pillars of social order. Hume's response to commercial aristocracy, which coincides perfectly with his skeptical epistemology, was to argue not that those who rule must truly be more rational, dispassionate, and virtuous than the rest of society, as Bolingbroke had insisted, but that they should seem to deserve a considerable degree of respect. With this in mind, Hume acknowledged the self-interested pursuits of the Whig oligarchy as an indisputable source of social improvement and prosperity. At the same time, he emphasized the most significant innovations of Walpole's administration, the system of public credit and the steps taken to maximize the power of the crown, as destabilizing forces that, sooner or later, would compel liberty to succumb to absolute power. The way to ward off this prospect, Hume argued, was not by any means to foment republican fantasies about civic selflessness and political rebirth but to avoid, as much as possible, any schemes that threatened habitual obedience to established authority.

While Hume regarded the moral authority of the aristocracy as a matter of public opinion, Smith attributed the deference paid to rank and fortune to popular delusions. Thus, whereas Hume stressed that social and political elites would command popular obedience as long as they maintained the appearance of superiority, Smith endlessly accentuated the morally misleading features of wealth and social position. Smith's preoccupation with the chimerical aspects of social and economic inequality resembles certain elements within Hume's philosophy, as well as particular components of Country ideology. Following Hume, Smith accepted the passion for private gain as a sign of the weakness of human reason and, therefore, rejected the classical republican conception of property as a platform for political authority. Much like Bolingbroke, moreover, he condemned avarice and ambition, the sins of the propertied few, as an inexhaustible source of moral decay and political incompetence. Consequently, in contrast to Hume's relatively unruffled resignation to the status quo, Smith went out of his way to underscore the corrupting effects of insatiable desire. As vehemently as any Country polemicist, Smith insisted that the universal pursuit of private advantage makes it impossible to draw any coherent distinction between the propertied elite and the propertyless majority.[17] Having accepted civic virtue as an extremely rare and, for all practical purposes, socially invisible quality, Smith endeavored to explain how society may flourish despite the moral infirmities that plague the powerful few as much or even more than they debilitate the powerless multitude.

As a contribution to some long-term debates about the historical evolution of liberal philosophy, this interpretation of Smith's "system of natural liberty" sets aside Marxian notions of bourgeois ideology—not to mention Hartzian preoccupations with the absence of aristocracy—in order to explore what happened when (for lack of a better word) "predemocratic" theorists recognized real aristocracy as an unattainable ideal. If, by pausing to look at this moment of recognition, I have discovered a somewhat greater degree of consistency in eighteenth-century British political theory than has previously been detected, it is because I have tried to treat Smith's work not as a bridge to nineteenth- or twentieth-century notions of liberal individualism, as once was commonly accepted, or as an effort to overcome republican complaints about commercial corruption, as Pocock and others suggest, but as the culmination of a decades-long debate about the moral and political dimensions of property ownership.[18] While this approach follows fairly directly from Pocock's "coat-trailing" comments on how hard it is to find unambiguous apologies for commerce in Anglo-American political philosophy, it deviates from his scholarship in significant ways.[19]

Because Pocock likes to cite the republican paradigm to explain everything from the reaction to the South Sea Bubble to the "immolation" of the Nixon administration, he tends to deprive the civic tradition of any historical or theoretical consequence.[20] Thus, even though Pocock's writings provide the starting point for this study, his conclusions on the relationship between classical republicanism and commercial ideology exemplify exactly what I am trying to avoid. According to Pocock,

> The [republican] paradigm rejects or modifies a number of wisdoms once conventional and still persistent. Since it presents the ideal of republican virtue as an ideological assault upon the Whig regime, it presents Scottish social theory as the latter's ideological defence; from which it follows that the delineation of commercial society was not a criticism of aristocracy, but a vindication of it in its Whig form.[21]

Certainly, phrases like "from which it follows" would only make sense if the historical relationships under investigation remained constant while all of the actors within those relationships changed. The trouble with this ahistorical approach is not merely that it reduces the republican tradition to a bag of static complaints that might be unpacked just as well by Sam

Ervin as by Henry Fielding.[22] Vaulting over the ages in this manner also obscures an otherwise apparent connection between the collapse of civic humanism as a program for political reformation and the rise of classical liberal thought.

Therefore, rather than pretending that ideological confrontations mimic logical equations and, on that basis, imagining that every critique must elicit a vindication, the approach I have adopted here presents the republican principles of the Country opposition as a specifically aristocratic formulation and, on that basis, presents Scottish political economy as an exploration of the moral and political limitations of commercial aristocracy. The advantages of this strategy are, on one hand, that it allows us to place the Country party's critique of commerce firmly within the context of aristocratic society and, on the other, that it saves us from having to transmogrify Smith's amazingly brief enumeration of the duties of the sovereign into an apology for the modern Whig regime.[23]

The inspiration for this interpretation lies in one of the great and glaring ironies of the eighteenth century. As a host of historians has lately observed, after 1688, the British aristocracy achieved an "unexampled" degree of prosperity, stability, cohesiveness, and power.[24] Against the old-fashioned image of an ever more marginalized aristocracy, recent studies of this period stress that the commercialization of aristocratic property provided an increasingly homogeneous nobility with the means to consolidate and improve their estates, control local politics and national legislation, and commission splendid country houses, gorgeous parks, magnificent city mansions, exquisite paintings, and similar marvels to celebrate their hallowed right to lord it over everybody else. However, at the very moment when these monuments to inequality seemed to express what David Cannadine has described as a "heightened sense of privilege and an extended sense of identity," eighteenth-century writers on politics and morality never stopped complaining about the moral failings of the most powerful members of British society.[25]

The irony here is that these complaints were not confined to satirists such as Mandeville, who aimed at elites because their conceits offered an easy target, or alarmists such as Bolingbroke, who genuinely regarded himself as a witness to national decline. Hume, the alleged apostle of commercial aristocracy, freely admitted that, though it was regrettable that the rulers of Great Britain relied so heavily on patronage and corruption, their moral shortcomings made it impossible for them to govern themselves and the nation in any other way.[26] And finally Smith, who celebrated eighteenth-century Britain as a "well governed," "civilized and thriving country," blessed with "a general plenty" sufficient to reach the "lowest ranks" of society, created a comprehensive theory of social and economic progress based on the conviction that political leaders cannot be expected to perceive, much less to promote, the public good.[27]

Because Smith scholars have generally failed to appreciate his preoccupation with aristocratic incompetence, they have chalked up his animadversions on those who occupied the top of the social hierarchy either to republican disdain for nobility or, more recently, to moral misgivings about the concentration of wealth in the hands of merchants and manufacturers rather than country gentlemen. Citing the many arguments Smith made in favor of agricultural investment and country living, as well as his contempt for the dissolute and wasteful behavior he detected in cities and towns, several scholars have downplayed the moral and political detachment displayed throughout the *Wealth of Nations* in order to highlight Smith's commitment to moral and political reform.[28] To the extent that they recognize Smith's misgivings about certain aspects of commercial development, these studies clearly provide a more complete understanding of the historical emergence of classical political economy. However, by exaggerating Smith's confidence in moral correction and political intervention, they obscure the cardinal purpose of his writings, which was to explain how the ubiquitous pursuit of personal advantage spontaneously advances the historical progress of opulence and, despite a few retrograde detours, generates a level of abundance adequate to offset even the most onerous instances of political abuse.

"Spontaneously" may strike Smith scholars as a reductionist reverberation of his undeserved reputation as a slavish apologist for free enterprise. I use it not because I hope to resurrect Smith as the Pollyanna of liberal political economy, but because I think it applies to his contention that purely self-interested individuals promote social prosperity without any knowledge of that objective, any concern for the public, or any intention to benefit anyone but themselves. In nineteenth- and twentieth-century political and economic theory, this contention has been used to defend limited government for the sake of individual liberty. In contrast, by placing Smith within the ideological context of the eighteenth century, I hope to show that his case for political nonintervention can be more accurately interpreted as a response to the moral contradictions of commercial aristocracy. More specifically, by juxtaposing the *Theory of Moral Sentiments* and the *Wealth of Nations* with Mandeville's defense of aristocratic depravity, Bolingbroke's distress about the decline of true nobility, and Hume's skeptical approach to political authority, I hope to show that Smith's insight into the advantages derived from the pursuit of private interest led him to abandon aristocratic assumptions about social hierarchy, but, in line with the limitations of eighteenth-century political theory, never inspired him to imagine that moral equality might be reconciled with the practice of politics. This study accordingly echoes earlier accounts of the way Smith "deflected," "severed," or, more recently, "emancipated" economics from political philosophy, but explains that move, not as an effort to accommodate what is vaguely known as the "human condition," but as an historically specific, essentially aristocratic response to the leveling effects of commercial development.[29]

Though this might seem like an appropriate place to emphasize the relevance of this study to our understanding of ongoing political and economic issues, one of the objects of this investigation is to locate republican ideology and classical political economy within the obviously archaic framework of aristocratic society. Consequently, against those scholars who imagine that a revival of civic virtue might somehow provide relief from the emptier aspects of present-day liberal democracy, the approach I take here underscores the eighteenth-century republican idealization of participatory liberty as an entirely antiquated rationale for social, economic, and political disparity.[30] Likewise, against those theorists who imagine that the *Wealth of Nations* might supply some insight into the "economic limits to politics" at the end of the twentieth century, this account indicates that Smith's case for limited government sprang from his conviction that ordinary human beings cannot be expected to perform as competent citizens, a conviction that can be traced to his failure to find a place for moral superiority within the public structures of modern commercial life.[31] This standpoint may reduce the subjects of this study to historical curiosities, but it suggests that, however much postmodernists may doubt the reality of social progress, the popular social movements of the past two hundred years have overturned the antidemocratic foundations of classical liberal political and economic thought.[32]

II

Thanks, But No Thanks:
Mandeville's Defense
of Court Whig Hypocrisy

ernard Mandeville, a Dutch physician who authored a *Treatise of Hypocondriak and Hysterick Passions*, is now mainly remembered, not for his contributions to medicine, but for his poem, "The Grumbling Hive, or Knaves Turn'd Honest," which was first issued as a six-penny pamphlet in London in 1705.[1] Although the poem aroused enough attention to elicit a pirated edition later that year, it did not provoke significant controversy until 1723, when it was reissued as part of a much larger volume under the title *The Fable of the Bees*. Along with a set of explanatory "Remarks," this book included an "Inquiry into the Origin of Moral Virtue," an "Essay on Charity and Charity Schools," and "A Search into the Nature of Society." These ambitious additions certainly indicate that Mandeville meant to create if not a sober system of moral philosophy then at least a respectable audience for his work.[2]

Like the "Remarks," the essays hammer home the message of the "Grumbling Hive," namely that it is vice rather than virtue that makes us sociable creatures and secures our preservation and prosperity. And like the poem itself, the essays never attempt to rise above the level of ironic observation. Instead, by exposing the hypocrisy involved in the pursuit of public virtue, and extolling the benefits derived from indulgence in private vice, they allege that virtue is as improbable as vice is inevitable. This allegation, which Mandeville presented in painstakingly provocative terms, was designed neither to indict nor to defend the viciousness of human nature. Instead, Mandeville aimed only to mock those moralists who imagined that a reformation of manners might restore humanity from its deplorable state of depravity to a society built on the principles of benevolence and virtue. Mandeville's move from "Dogrel" verse to relatively sophisticated prose was consequently not an attempt to develop an alternative code of social morality; it merely allowed him to expound his thesis twice, first as parody, then as farce.

That the 1723 edition of the *Fable* attracted widespread attention cannot be attributed entirely to the fact that Mandeville appended a few polished essays to the "Grumbling Hive." The connections he drew between private vices and social prosperity gained particular import in the furor that followed the South Sea Bubble of 1720. The spectacular rise and fall of the South Sea Company's scheme, first to assume the obligations of the national debt and then to rescue itself from that burden by inciting a storm of speculation, demonstrated, as nothing before, the political implications of commercial development. In the wake of the crash, social stability seemed to have been shifted from the province of government and placed in the hands of private individuals who had not the slightest concern about the social consequences of their self-interested pursuits. Moreover, when it was discovered, in the aftermath of the panic, that members of the government had connived to profit from the scheme, crowds of Country propagandists proclaimed that Robert Walpole, the principal minister of the Whig regime, had sold himself and the rest of the government into bondage to a "sinister money'd interest" that would soon transform instability into absolute tyranny.[3]

Walpole's response to the South Sea crisis did nothing but multiply the charges of corruption that were already pouring from the antigovernment press. While his opposition clamored for a full investigation into ministerial misconduct, stiff punishments for all those implicated in the scheme, and strong measures to regulate commercial and financial projects, Walpole protected powerful Whigs from prosecution, restored the confidence of the commercial interests, and exploited the disarray within the government to consolidate his personal power. To the Old Whig and Tory alliance, these actions stood out as milestones on the road to national destruction. Country writers accordingly warned that when government succumbs to the rule of avarice and ambition, corruption gradually overtakes the people as a whole. This diseased condition, which eighteenth-century writers typically equated with feminization, was commonly supposed to reduce the nation to such a level of submissive degradation that it would inevitably lead to foreign invasion. Commenting on this scenario, Mandeville observed:

> What is laid to the Charge of Luxury . . . is, that it increases Avarice and Repine: And where these are the reigning Vices, Offices of the greatest trust are bought and sold; the Ministers that should serve the Publick, both great and small, corrupted; and the Countries every moment in danger of being betray'd to the highest Bidders: And lastly, that it effeminates and enervates the People, by which Nations become easy Prey to the first invaders. (*Fable*, 1:115)

In light of Mandeville's assertion that the contagion of corruption unleashed by the Walpole regime ought to be attributed to "bad Politicks" rather than to bad morals, the opposition assumed, like many subsequent readers of the *Fable*, that his writings must have been designed to justify the economic and political abuses of the Whig oligarchy (*Fable*, 1:115). There is, in fact, a great deal of evidence that seems to support this point of view. Along with most Court Whigs, Mandeville earnestly defended the Glorious Revolution and the resulting balance of powers within the British Constitution. In keeping, moreover, with the mainstream of modern Whiggism, he dismissed civic humanist sermons against the growth of the national debt and the establishment of a large standing army. His complaints against highflying clergy, his support for religious toleration, and his objections to passive obedience likewise illustrate his affinity with Court Whig ideology.[4]

On a more general level, Mandeville's writings exhibit an anti-utopian aspect that definitely fell into line with Court Whig commitment to the status quo. "The Grumbling Hive" presents an obvious case in point:

> Then leave Complaints: Fools only strive
> To make a Great an Honest Hive T' enjoy the World's Conveniencies
> Be fam'd in War, yet live in Ease

Without great Vices is a Vain
EUTOPIA seated in the Brain. (*Fable*, 1:36)

In 1720, in "Free Thoughts on Religion," Mandeville argued in similarly anti-utopian terms: "To expect ministries without faults, and courts without vices, is grossly betraying our ignorance of human affairs . . . human life is itself a mixture of good and evil: no mortal can be compleatly happy, and none are so miserable, but they might still be worse."[5] A typical Court Whig pamphlet, published ten years later, echoed the prosaic sentiments sometimes expressed in Mandeville's work: "Since no Government in the World, no System of Polity that was ever invented, can be otherwise than imperfect, no Administration infallible, there will forever be Defects to be complained of, Mistakes to be rectify'd."[6] Lord Hervey, one of the most prolific propagandists for Walpole's administration, offered an equally complacent defense of the existing political order. Against Old Whig critics of the Whig regime, Hervey asserted that a genuine Whig is pledged to promote

> not Anti-monarchical, Republican Whig-principles, (Principles defective in Theory, and more extravagant when thought of with a Possibility of being reduced to practice;) not such chimerical Whig-principles as are imbibed from Eutopian Speculation, but only the honest and good Whig-principles, those of preserving a limited Monarchy in the Shape and Fashion we now enjoy it.[7]

Likewise, Hervey insisted,

> Things are very well as they are. Why stir them? It is with many parts of Policy, both in Government and Religion, as it is with some liquors, they will neither of them bear being shaken. . . . It is very ill-judged to run the risk of spoiling all that is clear and good, only to squeeze out a little more of what is bad.[8]

DISPLEASING THE COURT AS MUCH AS THE COUNTRY

Of course, Mandeville did not earn his reputation as the doyen of degradation by blandly affirming that every form of government has its faults. He argued not merely that political perfection is an impossible ideal, but, in a manner designed to disturb every section of the political spectrum, that national prosperity depends on profligate consumption. In order to make this claim, he began by extending the definition of luxury, which had traditionally been seen as the major source of political corruption, to include "every thing not immediately necessary to keep a Man alive" (*Fable*, 1:107). He knew that his readers would find this definition far too severe; he pointed out, however, that any other standard would make the line between genuine needs and subjective desires impossible to fix. After all, "the Comforts of Life are so various and extensive, that no body can tell what People mean by them." People may, for instance, worship in the same congregation, but "when they pray for their daily Bread, the Bishop includes several things that the Sexton does not think on" (*Fable*, 1:108).

From this rigorous premise, Mandeville elaborated two entirely unacceptable alternatives: on one hand, in order to approach the civic humanist dream of a virtuous polity, society would be obliged to make a courageous retreat into impoverished isolation; on the other, in order to enjoy the material comforts of commercial progress, it must resign itself to the wily rule of improvident desire.

> Frugality is like Honesty, a mean starving Virtue, that is only fit for small Societies of good peaceable Men, who are contented to be poor so they may be easy; but in a large stirring Nation, you may soon have enough of it. 'Tis an idle dreaming Virtue that employs no Hands, and therefore very useless in a trading Country, where there are vast Numbers that one way or another must all be set to Work. Prodigality has a thousand Inventions to keep People from sitting still, that Frugality would never think of; and as this must consume a prodigious Wealth, so Avarice again knows innumerable Tricks to rake it together, which Frugality would scorn to make use of. (*Fable*, 1:104–5)[9]

Mandeville's cynical vision was obviously as intolerable to Court Whig apologists for economic expansion as it was to civic humanist champions of moral reform. No Court Whig was inclined to accept moral emasculation as the price of commercial development; and, in spite of the homage they paid to frugality and self-restraint, Country propagandists were hardly prepared to push abject poverty as a precondition for moral renewal. Mandeville thus presented the Whig supremacy not with an ideological defense, but with a moral dilemma; moreover, he managed to accomplish this not by rejecting the principles of civic humanism, but by taking those principles to an intolerable extreme.

In keeping with his air of absolute asceticism, Mandeville never explicitly recommended a retreat from traditional civic (or Christian) ideals. On the contrary, throughout the *Fable*, which he recommended as a "Book of severe and exalted morality," he consistently argued that every individual ought to practice selfless dedication to the public good.

> I lay down as a first Principle, that in all Societies, great or small, it is the Duty of every Member of it to be good; that Virtue ought to be encouraged, Vice discountenenced, the Laws obey'd, and the Transgressors punished. . . . I defy my Enemies to disprove what I have advanced . . . that if I have shewn the Way to worldly Greatness, I have always without Hesitation preferr'd the Road that leads to Virtue. . . . When I say that Societies cannot be raised to Wealth and Power, and the Top of Earthly Glory, without Vices; I don't think that by so saying I bid Men to be vicious. . . . A Man may write on Poisons and still be an excellent Physician. (*Fable*, 1:407)

If Mandeville did not explicitly prescribe vicious conduct, he did define it as the key to social progress and, adding insult to impiety, endlessly applauded its tonic effects. In "A Search into the Nature of Society," which was designed to refute Shaftsbury's *Characteristics*, he maintained, like any upright moralist, that the "fewer Desires a Man has and the less he covets, the more easy he is to himself . . . the more he loves Peace and Concord . . . and the more he shines in real Virtue." But the trouble with such laudable attributes is that while they might "qualify a Man for the stupid Enjoyments of a Monastick Life," they would never incline anyone to engage in any significant form of social cooperation. Since we are, according to Mandeville, "ever pushing our Reason which way soever we feel Passion to draw it, and Self-love pleads to all human Creatures . . . to justify their Inclinations," it must be admitted that "it is impossible that Man, mere fallen Man, should act with any other View but to please himself." Society must therefore have evolved, not from the sources of human satisfaction, that is, from the "Amiable Virtues and Loving Qualities of Man, but on the contrary . . . [from] his Wants, his Imperfections, and the variety of his Appetites." After all, "Where a man has every thing he desires, and nothing to vex or disturb him, there is nothing can be added to his Happiness; and it is impossible to name a Trade, Art, Science, Dignity or Employment that would not be superfluous in such a Blessed State" (*Fable*, 1:346). Universal contentment would, in other words, obviate any need for productive interaction.

The fact that social relations arise from the natural efforts of individuals to supply their own physical needs and to gratify their selfish desires was, in Mandeville's view, sufficient to show that rational insight is inimical to civilization. From this he surmised that "neither the Friendly Qualities and kind Affections that are natural to Man, nor the real Virtues he is capable of acquiring by Reason and Self-denial are the Foundation of Society"; instead,

> What we call Evil in this World, Moral as well as Natural, is the grand Principle that makes us sociable Creatures, the solid Basis, the Life and Support of all Trades and Employments without Exception; that there we must look for the True Origin of all Arts and Sciences, and that the Moment Evil ceases, the Society must be spoiled, if not totally dissolved. (*Fable*, 1:402)

Since civilization seems, on these terms, to survive on unrelieved irrationality, it is hardly surprising that Mandeville rejected the epistemological assumptions of social contract theory. Though he maintained that his inquiry into the origin of society dealt strictly with "Man in a state of Nature," he stressed that he had in mind individuals living under established political authority.

> I hope the Reader knows that by Society I understand a body Politick, in which Man either subdued by Superior Force, or by Persuasion drawn from his savage State, is become a Disciplin'd Creature, that can find his own Ends in Labouring for Others, and where under one Head or other Form of Government each member is rendered subservient to the Whole, and all of them by cunning Management are made to act as One. (*Fable*, 1:347)

Mandeville did not undertake, as Hume did, a point by point refutation of Locke's explanation of the origin of government, but he plainly anticipated Hume's critique of the idea that political societies begin with rational consent. Just as Hume argued, in keeping with his concept of the primacy of passion, that governments are generally formed by violence and obeyed out of habit and custom, Mandeville maintained that political authority must have first been established, not by any appeal to reason, but by force or emotional persuasion. In contrast to Hume, however, Mandeville included in his account of political development the problematic notion that the members of society are "by cunning management" collected into an orderly political community. Along these lines, he alluded to "cunning Men" and "skilful Politicians," describing these undefined authorities as "Those who had undertaken to civilize Mankind." In view of his keen appreciation of human limitations, it is hard to determine who Mandeville imagined might have the wherewithal to accomplish this task: "Whoever would civilize men, and establish them into a Body Politick must be thoroughly acquainted with all the Passions and Appetites, Strengths and Weaknesses of their Frame, and understand how to turn their greatest Frailties to the Advantage of the Publick." (*Fable*, 1:208). It has been suggested that this puzzling argument must have been constructed to flatter the Walpole regime, but Mandeville himself explained, in his "Inquiry into the Origin of Honour," that no single set of "wary Politicians" provides society with effective civil and political institutions.[10]

> Among the things I hint at [wise laws and effective forms of government], there are very few that are the Work of one Man, or of one Generation; the greatest Part of them are the Product, the joynt Labour of several Ages . . . the Wisdom I speak of is not the Offspring of a fine Understanding, or of intense Thinking, but of a sound and deliberate Judgement, acquired from a long experience of Business and a multiplicity of Observations. By this sort of Wisdom, and Length of Time, it may be brought about that there shall be no greater Difficulty in governing a large City, than (pardon the lowness of the simile) there is in the weaving of Stockings. (*Fable*, 2:323)

So long as it is kept in mind that Mandeville's concept of the "skilful Politician" presupposes an historical evolution of civil and political customs and institutions, it is possible to reconcile his account of the rise of government with his general lack of faith in political capacity. Government, considered as the outcome of "long Experience" and a "multiplicity of Observations," requires neither spiritual sanction nor rational consent either to explain its inception or to legitimize its operations. Thus, by attributing political development to the "joynt Labour of several Ages," Mandeville managed to sidestep both the absolutism implied in the doctrine of divine right and the epistemological expectations of social contract theory.[11]

Insofar as he reduced government to the level of any well-made machine, Mandeville suggested, much to the consternation of Whigs as well as Tories, that debates over who should rule are ultimately insignificant. Certainly, he conceded, "the most knowing, the most virtuous, and the least self-interested Ministers are the best," but until such improbable people appear, the "Places can't stand open, the Offices must be served by such as you can get" (*Fable*, 2:323, 335). The most sensible policy is consequently "not to trust to any Honesty, but what is built on Necessity; for unhappy is the People, and their Constitution will ever be precarious, whose Welfare must depend on the Virtues and Consciences of Ministers." National government should therefore be "so wisely contriv'd, that every Man of middling Capacity and Reputation may be fit for any of the highest posts" (*Fable*, 2:323). Given an intricate system of "judicious Cheques," "every Officer's fidelity may be placed in so clear a Light, that, the moment he forfeits it, he must be detected. It is by these Arts that the weightiest Affairs, and a vast multiplicity of them, may be managed with Safety and Dispatch, by ordinary Men, whose highest good is Wealth and Pleasure" (*Fable*, 2:325). Likewise, in a passage that directly anticipates Hume's "science of politics," Mandeville maintained, "That is the best Constitution which provides against the worst Contingencies, that is armed against Treachery, Knavery and Deceit, and all the wicked Wiles of human Cunning, and preserves itself firm, and remains unshaken, though most men prove to be Knaves."[12]

Mandeville's case for a set of constitutional checks and against the Country party's call for moral reformation followed from his conviction that greed and self-seeking are as fundamental to political success as they are to economic improvement. Just as "Tradesmen are generally forc'd to tell Lies in their own Defence, and invent a thousand improbable Stories, rather than discover what they really get by their Commodities," a "polite Minister" procures and preserves his position first by soft-soaping the king and then by contracting out the defense of his policies to a motley array of minions. What struck Mandeville about this arrangement was not, of course, that it insulted the dignity of the crown and the morality of the ministry, but that it set up a division of labor that allowed government to function despite the moral infirmities of those in power. Thus, once the "finish'd Courtier," has bootlicked his way into office, keeping his position becomes an easy task.

> When a Favourite has once established himself in the good Opinion of his Master, it is easy for him to make his own Family, engross the King's ear, and keep every body from him, but his own Creatures. Nor is it more difficult . . . to turn out of the Administration every body that was not of his own bringing in. . . . As to the defeating and disappointing all the Envy and Malice [a prime minister is] generally attack'd with; if the Favorite was to do all that himself, it would certainly . . . require extraordinary Talents and a great Capacity . . . but this is the Province of his Creatures, a Task divided into a great Number of Parts; and every body that has the least Dependence upon . . . the Minister, makes it his Business and his Study, as it is his Interest, on the one hand, to cry up their Patron, magnify his Virtues and Abilities, and justify his Conduct; on the other, to exclaim against his Adversaries, blacken their Reputation, and play at them every Engine. (*Fable*, 2:332)

Mandeville's cynical commentary on the "skilful Courtier" and his obedient "Creatures" was obviously directed against the Walpole ministry. Mandeville did not, however, mean to imply that anyone should prefer the Opposition. Instead, aiming, as usual, to aggravate all sides, he reiterated his political neutrality.

> I don't think that, generally speaking, Prime ministers are much worse than their Adversaries, who, for their own Interest, defame them, and, at the same time, move Heaven and Earth to be in their Places. Let us look out for two Persons of Eminence . . . of contrary Parties; and . . . we shall always find, that whoever is uppermost and in great Employ, has the Applause of his Party; and if things go tolerably well, his Friends will . . . derive all his Actions from laudable Motives: The opposite Side can discover no virtues in him; they will not allow him to act from any Principles but his Passions; and if anything be done amiss, are very sure that it would not have happen'd if their Patron had been in the same Post. This is the Way of the World. (*Fable*, 2:336–37)

Having reduced factionalism to a petty squabble between self-seeking hypocrites, Mandeville characteristically proceeded to point out its practical value. His argument in favor of partisan politics, which reappeared in Hume's political writings and showed up again in the *Federalist Papers*, was that opposing factions allow ambition to counteract ambition. Thanks to the perpetual pursuit of personal interest, office holders are constantly scrutinized by "malicious Onlookers that envy them their places." The animosities among political "Antagonists, and the Quarrels between Parties," accordingly constitute a "considerable Part of the Nation's Security" (*Fable*, 2:334).

THE POLITICAL ECONOMY OF MORAL CORRUPTION

Given Mandeville's vision of government as a self-regulating system of vicious competition, it might seem plausible to assume that he adopted a somewhat similar approach to the economy and embraced the principle, if not the supposedly sunny standpoint of free market philosophy. But however much his suspicion of ministers and politicians may have inclined him to separate politics from morality, it never inspired him to sever polity from economy. Throughout his writings, he adopted a highly interventionist approach to economic exchange. Despite the pains he took to highlight the stupidity and incompetence of those who rule, he stressed that, in economic matters, "Every Government ought to be thoroughly acquainted with, and steadfastly to pursue the interest of the Country. And since "Good Politicians by dextrous Management," can "always turn and divert the Course of Trade which way they please . . . they'll keep a watchful Eye on the Balance of Trade in general" (*Fable*, 1:116).[13]

Like most mercantilists, Mandeville argued that economic activity ought to be strictly controlled not because such regulation would promote the prosperity of private individuals, but because it would maximize the power of the state. In other words, he conceived of wealth as a public rather than private good. This anti-individualistic aspect of Mandeville's mercantilist outlook is, it has been suggested, especially evident in his pitiless attitude toward the laboring majority of society. On the grounds that national prosperity depends on a steady supply of cheap and ready labor, Mandeville argued that working people should always remain ignorant, passive, and poor. Given the disparity between this cruel recommendation and his spirited defense of luxury spending, it has been argued that

Mandeville was more than willing to sacrifice the individual well-being of most members of society merely to maximize the conspicuous comforts enjoyed by the propertied few.[14] The problem with this argument is that by implying that Mandeville was more sympathetic to the rich than to the poor, it obscures the paradoxical premise of his work. Mandeville consistently condemned commercial civilization, however much he may have delighted in its discontents. Thus, when he celebrated the benefits derived from the consumption of luxury goods, he was by no means attempting to prove that there is, at least in respect to the rich, a natural coincidence between private and public advantage. On the contrary, his contention that private vices are public benefits defines the corruption of individuals, especially elites, as the driving force behind social progress.

In view of the inclination among present-day historians to focus on Mandeville's harsh commitment to majority ignorance and poverty, it should be emphasized that the general tendency of his analysis was to undermine the moral foundations of social stratification. He not only portrayed the rich as profligate parasites, indulging themselves at the expense of the laboring poor, he stressed that their ostensible superiority springs from tricks played on reason by avarice and ambition.

> Had the meanest and most unciviliz'd Peasant leave Incognito to observe the Greatest King for a fortnight; tho' he might pick out several things he might like for himself, yet he would find a great many more, which, if the Monarch and he were to change Conditions, he would wish for his part to have immediately redress'd or alter'd, and with Amazement he sees the King submit to. And again, if the Sovereign was to examine the Peasant in the same manner, his Labour would be insufferable, the Dirt and Squalor, his Diet and Amours, his Pastimes and Recreations would all be abominable; but then what Charms would he find in the Other's Peace of Mind, the Calmness and Tranquillity of his Soul? (*Fable*, 1:315–16)

Social hierarchy is here portrayed as mere appearance; the moral superiority that people naturally associate with social, economic, and political preeminence is reduced to a flimsy disguise. Thus, if kings were to trade places with peasants, they would quickly discover what would become one of the truisms most frequently repeated in commercial societies, namely, that the best things in life are free. Of course, Mandeville never expected anyone to honor this conviction; he held that however frequently people might proclaim that it is better to be "poor in spirit," they would always behave as if it is better to be rich in fact.

According to Mandeville, our tendency to overlook the reality behind the veil of social inequality stems from the way the "Force of Custom" inclines us to idealize those who stand at the top of the social scale. Along these lines, Mandeville observed that, "our Liking or Disliking of things chiefly depends on Mode and Custom, and the Precepts and Example of our Betters and such whom one way or another we think to be Superior to us" (*Fable*, 1:330). One of the paradoxical results of this perceived superiority is that the more fervently we believe in it, the less it approaches the truth. More specifically, the closer we come to the objects of our emulation, and the more successful we are at obtaining the things that mode and custom tell us are worth possessing, the less able we are to comprehend the sources of genuine satisfaction. Peasants are, from this standpoint, better off than kings because they are generally confined to the realm of necessity and thereby protected from the beguiling illusions of luxury and improvidence. In other words, the same operations of the passions that give rise to social distinctions and drive individuals to conform to the rule of fashion empties those distinctions of any rational content. The more substantial the differences between the highest king and the lowest of his subjects seem to be, Mandeville concluded, the less likely they are to withstand rational scrutiny.

> Was impartial Reason to be Judge between real Good and Real Evil, and a Catalogue made accordingly of the several Delights and Vexations differently to be met with in both Stations, I question whether the Condition of Kings would be at all preferable to that of Peasants, even as Ignorant and Laborious as I seem to require the latter to be. The Reason why the Generality of People would rather be Kings than Peasants is first owing to Pride and Ambition, that is deeply riveted in human Nature, and which to gratify we daily see men undergo and despise the greatest Hardships. Secondly, to the difference there is the Force with which our Affection is wrought upon as the Objects are either Material or Spiritual. Things that immediately strike our outward Senses act more violently upon our Passions than what is the result of . . . the dictates of the most demonstrative Reason, and there is a much stronger Bias . . . in the first than there is in the latter. (*Fable*, 1:316)

As usual, Mandeville's point was that material enjoyment is inseparable from moral decay; to his upper-class readers he said, in effect, "the poor are different from you and me": the fact that they will never inherit any portion of the earth provides them not merely with greater peace of mind, but, to the extent that they are impervious to excess, with a certain degree of moral supremacy. That the spiritual superiority of the poor goes largely unheeded is, Mandeville asserted, witness to our natural incapacity to discern the relatively faint dictates of reason amidst the noisy operations of the passions. From this vantage point, social distinctions are not an expression of any genuine merit or justifiable desert; quite the opposite, they demonstrate the deceptions induced by the capricious commands of mode and custom.[15] In short, the rich are deaf to the dictates of reason not because they are, like the poor, subject to the corrupting effects of physical deprivation, but because they are subject to the erratic and frequently foolish prescripts of fashion.

This argument, which was very nearly repeated by Adam Smith, illustrates how hard it was for eighteenth-century theorists to find a place for moral integrity within the hierarchical structure of commercial society. Mandeville, who obviously had no concept of what we describe as equal opportunity, maintained that the scope of individual appetite is limited only by accidents of birth or other twists of fate which either afford or fail to afford personal access to wealth and power. From this, he logically surmised that the only reliable division one can make between the rulers and the ruled, between the propertied elite and the propertyless majority, is that the former are more likely to be consumed by avarice, envy, and pride. The rich, in this context, clearly cannot be expected to promote the public interest or to practice the largess associated with nobility. In fact, the only positive role aristocrats can play is to waste their lives in thoughtless consumption and thereby provide employment for everyone else. Property here remains essential to social order, but rather than raising those who possess it above the rabble and rewarding them with some degree of autonomy, it subjects them to a morally debilitating plague of irrational needs and desires.

THE PARADOX OF COMMERCIAL ARISTOCRACY

To understand why Mandeville's paradox remained largely unresolved throughout the eighteenth-century, it is helpful to consider what is missing from his work. He did not advocate free trade; nonetheless, in his lack of faith in government, his preoccupation with the pursuit of self-interest, his insight into the benefits of factional competition, and his disdain for the pretensions of aristocrats, Mandeville seems to conform to many of the most familiar principles of liberal philosophy. However, his writings depart from liberal theory, or, more precisely, conventional accounts of liberal ideology, in that he never drew any correlation between private property and individual liberty. To Mandeville, the pursuit of individual wealth presents itself as a source of corruption rather than rational decision-making, because it springs from fantastic illusions about personal gratification. Although the individuals who find themselves trapped in these illusions naturally and unwittingly contribute to national prosperity, they clearly do not, in Mandeville's view, understand their real interests or enjoy any degree of self-determination. They are, on the contrary, blind to their interests because they are enslaved by insatiable desire.

Subsequent theorists, particularly Hume and Smith, would soften these conclusions by emphasizing the pursuit of private advantage as the surest route to social refinement and general prosperity, but, as aristocratic thinkers, they freely conceded that the desire for personal gain garbled aristocratic conceptions of social hierarchy. Aristocrats are, after all, supposed to deserve position and prestige because they are genuinely better than those below them, not because their ignoble activities pay off in the long run for the rest of society. Hume, Smith, and like-minded moralists could not, consequently, solve the problem of self-interest by defining the natural effort to better one's own condition as a socially acceptable "interest," rather than a morally corrupting "passion."[16] Moral neutrality might have presented itself as a tolerable attitude if any of these thinkers had lived in a society shaped by ideas about moral equality, but an aristocratic system certainly cannot accommodate neutral terms.

The dilemma Mandeville's work posed within the context of the eighteenth century helps to remind us of what might be described as the "fallacy of political theory," that is, the tendency among historians of political thought to imagine that the development of their subject and, in some cases, history itself must reach an impasse if significant philosophical questions remain unresolved. This tendency proceeds, not only from a propensity to exaggerate the importance of political philosophy (for example, because Locke argued in favor of individual liberty, the American Revolution occurred), but also from a largely unexamined assumption that the purpose of political theory must be to iron out the insupportable aspects of social reality. However, without denying that political theory sometimes functions as apology, we simply have no reason to suppose that Hume, Smith, or any other theorist found a way out of the moral dilemma Mandeville found at the core of commercial society.

Dropping ideas about problem-solving makes it easier to appreciate the political pessimism of Mandeville's work. On one hand, he affirmed the traditional conviction that society must be divided between rich and poor, the few and the many. On the other, he opened a gulf between property ownership and moral capacity that deprived the higher-ups within the social hierarchy of any coherent claim to political power. In Mandeville's writings, property, which republicans had defined as a platform for moral autonomy and political authority, serves as a symbol of individual servility. In refusing to exempt the propertied minority from the degrading effects of unmet need, Mandeville very deliberately universalized the inferior moral status which had previously been reserved for the lower ranks. While this "first shall be last" mentality may have conformed to Christian ideas about the true relationship between wealth and poverty, Mandeville clearly aimed to underline the contradictory nature of commercial aristocracy, not to suggest that the propertied few ever would or could learn to discipline their vulgar and obvious desires.

Since Mandeville's thesis muddled the distance between kings and peasants and made it hard to tell prime ministers apart from common thieves, it accomplished his over-riding goal and enraged respectable persons of every political stripe. But as provoking as his portrait of British society must have been to Walpole and his supporters, it was an abomination to the civic-minded critics of the Whig regime. The most abhorrent aspect of the *Fable*, as it was read by Country writers such as Bolingbroke, Fielding, Pope, and Gay, was not only that it seemed to delight in the depravity of their day but that it upset the seemingly unassailable argument that moral corruption, especially the corruption of the elite, must end in social disarray.[17] Along these lines, for example, Fielding warned that, while the prodigal habits of the rich and the powerful would probably never provoke the collapse other writers described as imminent, the "vast Torrent of Luxury which of late Years hath poured itself into this Nation" would, if measures were not taken against it, progressively pass from the top to the bottom of the social hierarchy and eventually infect the common people with aspirations entirely out of keeping with their station. Against the idea that private vices promote general prosperity, Fielding insisted that luxury and dissipation could not be walled within the highest ranks.

I aim not here to satirize the great, among whom luxury is probably rather a moral than a political evil. But Vices no more than Diseases will stop with them; for bad habits are as infectious by example, as the Plague itself by Contact. In free countries, at least, it is Branch of Liberty claimed by the People to be as wicked and as profligate as their Superiors. Thus while the Nobleman will emulate the Grandeur of a Prince; and the Gentleman will aspire to the proper State of the Nobleman; the Tradesman steps from behind his Counter into the vacant Place of the Gentleman. Nor does the Confusion end here: It reaches the very Dregs of the People, who aspiring still to a Degree beyond that which belongs to them, and not being able by the Fruits of honest Labour to support the State which they affect, they disdain the Wages to which their Industry would entitle them; and abandoning themselves to Idleness, the more simple and poor-spirited betake themselves to a State of Starving and Beggary, while those of more Art and Courage become Thieves, Sharpers, and Robbers.[18]

Of course, Mandeville never invested the elite with this degree of moral authority. On the contrary, in contrast to the Country conviction that the improvidence of the commercial aristocracy would bankrupt society, he maintained that the "torrent of Luxury" unleashed by their avarice and ambition produced unprecedented plenty. At the same time, against the objection that the "very Dregs of the People" would become as "wicked and profligate as their Superiors," he identified ignorance, fear, and poverty as the most effective means to prevent the majority from slipping into indolence, thriftlessness, and crime. Having thereby relieved the aristocracy of any duty to show the common people how to maximize their industry, he found a way to explain how society may prosper even when its wealthiest and most powerful members find themselves trapped in what Bolingbroke depicted as "imaginary poverty," or obsessed by what Hume defined as the "feverish, empty amusements of luxury," or lost in what Smith described as the "wanton" and "disorderly pursuit of pleasure."[19] Mandeville elaborated this explanation, not by inventing any novel moral theory or science of society, but by reducing the Country party's lexicon of virtues—independence, providence, self-abnegation, and civic spirit—to a blueprint for the eradication of every last speck of material satisfaction. Then, to top it off, Mandeville sang every Country song about national corruption without ever insinuating that history or providence might provide an escape into a more tolerable age.

In presenting this all too detailed picture of commercial aristocracy, Mandeville pinpointed, remarkably early on, the most painful drawback of the Country party's critique of Court Whig supremacy, which was that Country propagandists could not articulate any alternative to commercial progress. This failure, which is explored in Chapter 3, serves to explain why Mandeville's system aroused such consternation and, as Adam Smith put it, "made so much noise in the world." When Smith reflected on the *Fable of the Bees* more than fifty years after it was originally published, he was accordingly obliged to admit that "howsoever destructive this system may appear, it could never have imposed upon so great a number of persons, nor have occasioned so general an alarm among those who are friends of better principles, had it not, in some respects, bordered on the truth" (*TMS*, 313). Similarly, Smith censured Mandeville, not because the *Fable* had brought more vice into the world than it might have otherwise encountered, but because "Dr. Mandeville . . . taught that vice, which arose from other causes, to appear with more effrontery, and to avow the corruption of its motives with a profligate audaciousness which had never been heard of before" (*TMS*, 314).

Smith's disapproving comments on Mandeville's writings show how misleading it can be to imagine that either author meant to construct some amoral "science of society." In a recent study, for example, E. G. Hundert interprets the *Fable* as part of a larger effort to invent an "explanation of sociability, and thus of moral standards, in a vocabulary shorn of moralized concepts." Mandeville's "naturalization of pride," according to Hundert, "came to be accepted as methodologically prescriptive for an entire program of social inquiry." Citing Jeremy Bentham's assertion that Mandeville had "broken the chains of ordinary language, " Hundert concludes, "It is a fitting paradox for so paradoxical an author that Mandeville's project of establishing a science of unsocial yet socialized man on the ruins of an exhausted language of morals should have been of such signal importance to the inheritors of this tradition."[20]

Without denying either the weight of Mandeville's impact on subsequent theorists or the many convincing arguments contained in Hundert's work, I think that this reading of Mandeville's intentions misses his main objective, which was, as he insisted in reply to his critics, to entertain his audience. This is not to imply that Mandeville was superficial or unserious; on the contrary, his very serious approach to morality is exactly what makes his work so consistently funny. The methodological prescription for successful parody is, after all, that it must be profound. Mandeville's commitment to comedy, which, given the sheer length of the *Fable*, certainly cannot be doubted, required him to deal with live issues, apposite social questions, genuine moral concerns. If Mandeville's reflections on social development were "shorn of moralized concepts," his witticisms, as he well knew, would not be entertaining; his jokes would just fall flat. In this respect, the notion that Mandeville would try to build anything on the "ruins of an exhausted language of morals" simply fails to capture his satirical purpose. By the time Bentham read Mandeville, perhaps the "chains of ordinary language," about selfishness had been broken (at least until they were mended in the martyrdom of John Stuart Mill). But, as illustrated by the controversy incited by the *Fable*, as well as its author's delighted response to that reaction, the idea that private vices benefit the public clearly transgressed the boundaries of acceptable morality and thus solicited charges such as Smith's complaints about "audacious effrontery," precisely the result that Mandeville hoped to achieve.[21]

In keeping with the insupportable nature of the "rustic Doctor's" thesis, Bolingbroke, Hume, and Smith, who, without question, counted themselves among the "friends of better principles," were all duly alarmed by Mandeville's system of morality, and all of them felt compelled to respond to the correlation he drew between private depravity and public prosperity, individual viciousness and social development. Without understating the expanse between the "Grumbling Hive" and the *Wealth of Nations*, however, an examination of Bolingbroke's campaign to reform the aristocracy, Hume's fears about vanishing respect for nobility, and Smith's contention that the rulers of Great Britain should resign themselves to their own mediocrity shows that none of these writers managed to find a place for genuine moral superiority and, therefore, competent political authority within the framework of modern commercial life. What follows is accordingly designed to show how Bolingbroke, Hume, and Smith approached the problem of political leadership given, on one hand, Mandeville's insight into the oxymoronic aspects of commercial aristocracy and, on the other, the practical example of the modern Whig regime.

III

Bolingbroke's Search
for a Patriot King

I f any collection of writings can be upheld as the antithesis of the *Fable of the Bees*, it is the work of Henry St. John, Viscount Bolingbroke, the leading critic of the Whig ascendancy. In contrast to Mandeville's gleeful gibes about getting and spending, Bolingbroke warned that the uncontrolled pursuit of private interest would upset the delicate balance of powers within the constitution, undo the happy conclusion of the Glorious Revolution, undermine every defense against foreign invasion and, ultimately, sink the entire country into impoverished desolation. A host of economic developments in post-Revolutionary England, including onerous taxes on land, the establishment of public credit, the rise of the great chartered companies, and a rage of stock speculation, set the stage for Bolingbroke's scenario. The villain of the piece was, of course, the Great Man, Bluff Bob, the Poet's Foe, Robert Walpole.[1]

Though the length of Walpole's leadership (1721–42) stands out as the most telling comment on the efficacy of the opposition, Bolingbroke's campaign against the ministry was both cogent and consistent. From his first contributions to *The Craftsman* to his late essay on "The Idea of a

Patriot King," Bolingbroke blazed away at the decidedly ambiguous ratio-nale behind Walpole's program of patronage and corruption. This pro-gram, which included fixing elections, doling out military, ecclesiastic, and civil positions, and extending various perquisites to hangers-on and henchmen, was designed, its defenders said, to help the Crown hold its own against the increasing concentration of property and power in the Commons. But no matter what kind of constitutional finery the system might have worn in the government press, the fact that it turned on greed and self-seeking could not be disguised. Thus, with what might have been a sidelong glance at the *Fable of the Bees*, Bolingbroke derided Walpole's ministry as depravity teaching by examples.[2] "The minister," he declared in "The Idea of a Patriot King," "preaches corruption aloud and con-stantly, like an impudent missionary of vice: and some there are who not only insinuate, but teach the same."[3] Likewise, in a letter to Lord Chesterfield, Bolingbroke denounced the Mandevillean cast of the minis-ter's methods: "Not content to neglect, he ridiculed every public virtue. Not content to ridicule them, he established every opposite vice, and took off that last remnant of shame which might have been improved to check, and under a better administration, reform them."[4]

Bolingbroke's bitter reaction to Walpole's system stemmed from his historical understanding of the political structure perfected by the Glori-ous Revolution. Along with Whigs both Old and New, Bolingbroke cele-brated the Revolution Settlement of 1688 because it defined precisely the proper boundaries among the monarchical, aristocratic, and democratic elements of government. It liberated the Crown from unseemly schemes to fortify its prerogative, permitted the Lords to fulfill their juridical func-tion, and allowed the Commons to stand up for the people as a whole. Thanks to this exquisite arrangement, Bolingbroke wrote, "No estate has a separate, contradictory interest. . . . The commons have discarded the badge of servitude, the crown has relinquished claims of absolute superi-ority."[5] Likewise, against the Court Whig proposition that the power of Parliament had grown too great after 1688, Bolingbroke maintained that the Revolution had reinforced the "true foundations of kingly authority. . . . The throne is now established, not on the narrow and sandy founda-tion of courtcraft, and unconstitutional expedients, but on the popularity of the prince, and the universal affection of his subjects."[6]

While Bolingbroke strategically emphasized his attachment to the monarchy, he dwelt on the autonomy of Parliament as the only true guarantor of British liberty. In the *Craftsman*, for example, presenting

what he described as "extracts from the FREEHOLDER'S Political Cate-
chism," Bolingbroke asked, among other questions, "Is not the Justice of
a King sufficient Security for the Liberty of a People?" To which he had
"T.M., a Freeholder of Great Britain," reply:

> A. The People ought to have more Security for all, that is valuable
> in the World, than the Will of a mortal and fallible Man. A King of
> Britain may make as many Peers, and such, as he pleaseth; and
> therefore the last and best Security for the Liberties of the People, is
> a House of Commons genuine and independent.[7]

Virtually all of Bolingbroke's observations on the framework of British
government were designed to show that Walpole's attempts to secure the
submission of the Commons by soliciting the self-interest of its members
presented a clear and present danger to the integrity of the constitution
and, consequently, the safety and stability of British society. In the first
place, Bolingbroke argued, far from strengthening the pillar of royal prerogative, political dependence would gradually bankrupt the king, as well
as his subjects and would, as poverty spread, produce precisely what it
was supposed to preclude. "Such as serve the Crown for Reward may in
Time sacrifice the Interest of their Country to their *Wants*. . . . *Greediness*
of public Money may produce a slavish *Compliance*, as long as the Crown
can pay; and Mutiny when it cannot."[8]

The risk inherent in Walpole's endeavors to employ avarice and ambition to meet his aims was, according to Bolingbroke, not only that it
would ultimately deprive the king of all of his loyal servants, but that it
would induce insatiable passions and uncontrollable cravings which
would seep from the political elite down to the lowest reaches of society.
The monarch who stoops to secure his goals by bribery, Bolingbroke
argued in the misogynist terms of republican ideology, "subjects Himself
to the arbitrary Will and fanastical government of "*Prostitutes*," and, in
so doing, ignites a general contagion of immorality.

> Such Proceedings, when generally known, debauch the Morals of a
> whole People. The *same Depravity and Corruption*, soon find their
> way from a Court to a Cottage; and in Proportion to the Distance,
> is to be traced in a greater or less degree through every private Fam-
> ily, so that in a very short time the very name of virtue may be lost
> in such a Kingdom.[9]

CIVIC VIRTUE AND ARISTOCRATIC RULE

Bolingbroke derived the fabric for his interpretation of the consequences of corruption from Machiavelli's teachings on public spirit, constitutional stability, and national decline.[10] Along with Old Whigs and neo-Harringtonians such as John Trenchard and Thomas Gordon, authors of *Cato's Letters*, Bolingbroke cited Machiavelli to show that modern Whiggism threatened the original principles contained in the constitution, principles which had been revived, to a great degree, by the Glorious Revolution, but which might be or, perhaps, had been corrupted by Walpole's depraved indifference to public virtue. Corruption, Bolingbroke asserted, naturally occurs over time, but the rate at which it spreads throughout society depends on the strength of public morality which, in turn, depends on the moral stature of the ruling elite. Thus, in the "Power of the Prince," clearly patterned, like the "Idea of a Patriot King," after Machiavelli's writings, Bolingbroke praised the restorative effects of previous revolutions, but suggested, nevertheless, that "ancient liberty" had never been entirely revitalized.

> Machiavel, in his political discourses, lays down this proposition; that no government can long enjoy liberty, unless it be frequently brought back to its first principles. It is the nature of all government to degenerate. As it grows older, it gradually deviates and flies farther from its first intention, which is singly the advantage of society; till at last it attains such a degree of corruption, that its order becomes entirely inverted; and that institution, by which the prince was first only the servant of the public, obliges the public to be slaves to the prince. . . . The various revolutions in this kingdom have, in great measure, answered this end. They have purged off the luxuriances of power; and though few of them have gone so deep as to bring us back to the primitive purity of our constitution, yet they have still preserved us a free people, when liberty is lost in almost every part of Europe.[11]

Bolingbroke's qualifications about "primitive purity" allowed him to celebrate the Glorious Revolution as an admirable renewal without obliging him to affirm the New Whig notion that British liberty had made its first appearance in 1688.[12] To those who mistook his preoccupation with the strength of the constitution for doubts about the felicity of the Revo-

lution and concluded that his opposition could be more accurately described as sedition, Bolingbroke answered that his aim was not to undo
but to uphold the principles professed by every patriot. In fact, Bolingbroke argued, anyone who chose to be less vigilant would undermine the
settlement reached at the Revolution and starve liberty by neglect.[13]

> The sum therefore of all of these discourses ought to be, that we
> should not stop short in so important a work. It was begun at the
> revolution; but he who thinks it was perfected then, or hath been
> perfected since, will find himself very much mistaken. The founda-
> tions were laid then. We proceeded for some time after that, like the
> Jews in rebuilding their temple; we carried on the holy work with
> one hand, and held our swords in the other to defend it. That dis-
> traction, that danger is over, and we betray the cause of liberty with-
> out any color of excuse, if we do not complete the glorious building,
> which will last to ages yet remote, if it be once finished, and will
> moulder away and fall into ruins, if it remain longer in this unfin-
> ished state.[14]

What placed the constitution in such immediate danger of dissolution
was, in Bolingbroke's view, not only that Walpole had adopted the most
pernicious methods of government, but that many of those who had the
most to lose from the ministry had surrendered to the lowest temptations,
and some had sunk so low that they had become apologists for their own
ruination. That upstarts and new moneyed men would be taken in by
Walpole's machinations seemed to Bolingbroke make some sense; he
found it hard to believe, however, that the upper-class would crumble
under the minister's commands.

> There is surely but too much reason to suspect that the enemies of
> our constitution may attempt hereafter to govern by corruption;
> when it is pleaded for and recommended as a necessary expedient of
> government, by some men, of all ranks and orders; not only by
> professed hirelings, who write that they may eat, but by men who
> have talked and written themselves already out of their native obscu-
> rity and penury: not only by these, but by men whose birth, educa-
> tion, and fortune, aggravate their crime and their folly; and by men
> whose peculiar obligations to preach up morality should restrain

them, at least from being the preachers of an immorality, above all
others, abominable in its nature and pernicious in its effects.[15]

As indicated here, Bolingbroke held that those who are distinguished
by "birth, education, and fortune" are by nature fated to fulfill distinct
moral duties, the first of which is to safeguard liberty by promoting general morality and placing their talents at the service of their country. "He
who considers the universal wants, imperfections, and vices of his kind,
must agree," Bolingbroke argued, "that men were intended not only for
society, but to unite in commonwealths, and to submit to laws." But
despite the connections between the defects of human nature and the
establishment of government, and despite the opportunities this establishment creates for abuses of power, the truth remains, "that all men are
directed, by the general constitution of human nature, to submit to government, and that some men are in a particular manner designed to take
care of that government on which the common happiness depends." In
other words, the same frailties which give rise to government dictate that
the few who can transcend ordinary imperfection must take charge of
everybody else.

> Since men are so apt, in every form of life and every degree of
> understanding, to act against their interest and their duty too, with-
> out benevolence to mankind, or regard to the Divine Will; it is
> more incumbent on those who have this benevolence and this regard
> at heart, to employ all the means that the nature of government
> allows, and that rank, circumstances of situation, or superiority of
> talents, give them, to oppose evil and promote good government;
> and contribute thus to preserve the moral system of the world at that
> point of perfection at least, which seems to have been prescribed for
> it by the great Creator of every system of beings.[16]

Bolingbroke's understanding of the political role of the elite within the
natural course of things formed the crux of his campaign against commercial modernity. Translated into the particulars of the British system, Bolingbroke's vision of social stratification issued from the conviction that
certain men are born to lead because their property attaches them to the
interests of their country, noble birth provides them with a sense of civic
duty, inheritance allows them to cultivate their talents, and rank places
them before the public eye. Walpole's Mandevillean methods of manag-

ing parliament would sabotage the moral and material framework of this system by transforming property from a protection against corruption into an agent and object of prostitution, scrambling every social distinction in an undignified free-for-all.

While Bolingbroke sometimes portrayed this prospect as a distant possibility and other times suggested that it had very nearly come to pass, he always regarded the notion that those who had been chosen to represent the nation might be led by the most trivial enticements to ignore their "peculiar obligations" with incredulous disdain. "For how," he asked in *The Craftsman*,

> can we *Englishmen* suppose, that Men qualify'd by their *Fortunes* as well as their *Abilities*, should ever be influence'd by *Bribery, Gain, or Pensions*, to throw down the enclosures of their Constitution, and draw upon themselves a *universal Odium*, by acting in Opposition to the *Persons*, whom they pretend to represent; and, what is more mean and inglorious, divest themselves of their Reason, Understanding, and all Regard to Posterity, and condescend to be led, by a *great wicked Minister*, thro' all the *intricate Mazes* and *dirty Passages*, which *private Interests, insatiable Lusts, and unruly Ambition* shall suggest to him, to the Destruction of their Country in the End?[17]

That Walpole had grown into such a grave threat to the independence of parliament, against the force of law and the manners of the nation, could not be ascribed to diabolical genius; rather, Bolingbroke argued, the minister's astonishing success sprang from the evolution, in the aftermath of the Revolution, of an entirely new source of corruption, public funding of the national debt. With the establishment of public credit, Walpole gained access to what seemed to be almost unlimited means to expand the military and augment the civil list. By gambling on the credit of burdensome taxes and peddling the interest of the public to private investors, Walpole had managed, according to Bolingbroke, to double his means of corruption. On one hand, by exhausting the resources of the gentry, particularly through taxes on land, the minister deprived those who might have otherwise resisted of any asylum from seduction. On the other, by drawing newly made speculators into the government, he gained a gang of compliant allies. Thus, in "A Dissertation on Parties," Bolingbroke described what a "veteran sharper" might accomplish were he supplied with a fantastic combination of taxes and debt:

> He may corrupt men with their own spoils, and bribe even those
> whom he reduced by his clandestine practices to that penury which
> could alone make them capable of being bribed or, when he hath to
> do with men of another character, (for no rank alone will be sufficient to raise them, in such an age, above the most direct and prostitute corruption,) he may bribe them by a whisper . . . and secure
> them by a participation of the same fraud and the same profit.[18]

Along with public credit, Bolingbroke cited stock trading as an integral part of Walpole's dastardly plot against the natural hierarchy of British society. Having transformed the treasury into a "mystery of iniquity," Walpole set in motion the "artificial wheel of credit," creating a new and precarious type of property that assumed the form of "paper estates." As insubstantial as these newfangled estates may have been, Bolingbroke complained, they allowed the "meanest grubs on earth [to raise] themselves by stockjobbing, to the rank and port of noblemen and gentlemen" and, simultaneously, encouraged "noblemen and gentlemen [to] debase themselves to their meanness, and acquire the same spirit, by following the same trade."[19] But the overall effect of stockjobbing, in Bolingbroke's opinion, was not only that it undid the real distinctions between "gentlemen" and "grubs," but that it seemed to convert wealth into poverty and, by means of this magic, induce those who ought to have been indifferent to succumb to illusions of infinite need.

> Public want or general poverty . . . will lay numbers of men open
> to attacks of corruption; so private wealth will have the same effect,
> especially where luxury prevails, on some of those who do not feel
> the public want; for there is imaginary as well as real poverty. He
> who thought himself rich before, may begin to think himself poor,
> when he compares his wealth . . . with [that of] men he hath been
> used to esteem, and perhaps justly, far inferior to himself in all
> respects. He who would have been ashamed to participate in fraud,
> or to yield to corruption, may begin to think the fault venial, when
> he sees men who were far below him, rise above him by fraud and
> by corruption; when he sees them maintain themselves by these
> means in an elevation which they could not have acquired by the

contrary virtues if they had them. . . . Thus . . . poverty and wealth combine to facilitate the means and the progress of corruption.[20]

To underscore the irrationality of acquisitive behavior, Bolingbroke compared the disordered temper of stockjobbing to the fanatical force of faction. Just as stock trading reduced those who should have been promoting general prosperity to perpetual anxiety about their personal affairs, factional conflict convinced otherwise rational participants in the political sphere to place partisan objectives above the public good. In language that might be described as an anti-anticipation of both Hume and Madison, Bolingbroke argued that, as much as stockjobbing threatened to choke the vitality of commerce,

> the spirit of it is not yet extinguished . . . though the spirit of stockjobbing be to that of trade, what the spirit of faction is to that of liberty. The tendency of both is to advance the interests of a few worthless individuals at the expense of the whole community. The consequence of both, if they ever happen to prevail to the ruin of trade and liberty, must be, that harpies will starve in the midst of imaginary wealth; and that the children of faction, like the iron race of Cadmus, will destroy one another.[21]

The same fear of social and political upheaval that inspired Bolingbroke's case against stock speculation and factional competition led him to denounce the great chartered companies that had mushroomed under Walpole's hand. By protecting and promoting the interests of monopolistic corporations, particularly the South Sea Company, Walpole had reduced commerce to one more "narrow intrigue" to further his "sinister designs" against the commonweal.[22] With this in mind, Bolingbroke advocated freedom of trade not by any means because he conceived of the economy as a self-regulating system, but because Walpole's preferential policies seemed to make the wheels of commerce turn on private rather than public prosperity. Thus, in *The Craftsman*, in a letter from "Charles Freeport," Bolingbroke charged that Walpole's connivance with the governors and directors of the major trading companies thwarted the industry of lesser tradesmen and merchants, exacerbated poverty with increased unemployment, and, worst of all, transformed commerce, which should have been a source of general plenty, into yet another fountain of corrupt and uncontrollable power.

In fine, to what dangerous uses may these Companies be made subservient, by corrupt and enterprising Ministers? . . . Is not the Common-Seal of all Companies, by which they may at any time raise what Sums of Money they Please, equal to a power of Coining, or taxing their fellow Subjects; which even the King himself cannot do, without the Consent of Parliament? Have not all Ministries an influence over those Companies, and may they not by their means be able to influence the Elections of every City, and Trading Town in England? and what may we not justly apprehend from such formidable, complicated Power, which may, at one time or other, destroy our happy Constitution?[23]

Bolingbroke's case against monopolistic companies was clearly not an effort to liberate economic interaction from political control. On the contrary, his complaint was that under Walpole the heroic "gentlemen," that is, the born statesmen who should have been overseeing the material well-being of the nation had been supplanted by self-interested "grubs."

REPUBLICAN IDEALISM AND POLITICAL DESPAIR

After years of haranguing the nation to pay some mind to Walpole's schemes to dissolve the constitution in a deluge of courtcraft and financial manipulation, Bolingbroke seems to have concluded that the Country party's efforts to stem the tide of corruption were, if not hopeless, then at least unlikely to succeed. In his final essays, he turned his expectations away from his contemporaries and suggested that Britain's salvation would have to come either from some future generation or, much more improbable, from the preternatural emergence of a "Patriot King." Bolingbroke's composition on this miraculous monarch, a follow-up to his essay "On the Spirit of Patriotism," includes a list of Walpole's transgressions against his people and posterity which infers that the minister had driven the country so far down the path of iniquity that, having reached the intersection between universal anarchy and absolute monarchy, the only way that Britain might find its way back to safety and liberty would be to bend to the example and direction of an ideal prince, a figure Bolingbroke designates as the "most uncommon phenomena in the physical or moral world."[24]

Isaac Kramnick has criticized Bolingbroke's rhapsodic remarks in "A

Patriot King" as a digression from his otherwise consistent assumption that the state of public morality depends on the social and economic conditions prevailing at any given time. What separates this essay from the main body of Bolingbroke's work, according to Kramnick, is that it proposed that an ideal ruler might set a moral example which would be sufficient to raise his entire society from the depths of depravity and, thereby, restore the political system to its original purity, without regard to economic practices or property relations. Bolingbroke thus forsook his Harringtonian perception of corruption as the outcome of specific institutional and economic arrangements in favor of a Machiavellian interpretation of political degeneration as a moral process which, though it naturally occurs over time, might be mitigated by a rededication to original ideals. More specifically, against his own comparatively pragmatic reading of the way public credit and stockjobbing had undermined the economic underpinnings of the constitution, he sought a strictly idealistic refuge from the progress of national decline.[25]

As insightful as this reading is, it tends to underestimate Bolingbroke's preoccupation with government as the vanguard of public morality. In line with his notion that some men are simply born to lead, Bolingbroke always measured the moral condition of society by the moral caliber of the ruling elite. In his tributes to Queen Elizabeth, for instance, he insisted that the glory of her age arose from the fact that she was, by "Nature, as well as art," blessed with such a degree of wisdom and virtue that she overcame every circumstance and managed, despite costly wars, factional intrigue, religious conflict, and economic distress, to bring the constitution to a point of stability which it had never reached before.[26] Likewise, when he argued that corruption cascades from the highest court to the meanest cottage, he proceeded from the premise that those who occupy the top of the social hierarchy are naturally and entirely responsible for the moral and political integrity of society as a whole. In short, in line with his general conception of political leadership as the key to common morality, prior to the material framework of society, Bolingbroke's trickle-down theory of virtue and corruption appeared everywhere in his work. In the *Craftsman*, he accordingly expressed precisely the same idealism as is displayed in the "Patriot King": "A Government may be conducted with the greatest Security, without employing these *pecuniary Arts* . . . ; for a *wise Administration* will always stand on its own Legs, and support itself without the Assistance of *Gold*. It can raise a whole People, almost from a State of *Barbarity*, to the Heighth of Greatness and heroick Virtue."[27]

Charging ministers and politicians with this level of moral authority was more than a strategic way to raise the stakes against Walpole. Bolingbroke's highflying hopes of the glories that might be accomplished by a "wise Administration," as well as a "Patriot King," illustrate his conviction that those who stand at the head of government should deserve to stand at the pinnacle of society. As much pressure as public credit and stockjobbing might have placed on the material foundations of the traditional social hierarchy, these were, in Bolingbroke's view, insufficient to explain the ostensible decay of the constitution and the paralysis which had apparently overtaken the British aristocracy. An authentic aristocrat cannot, after all, pretend to be a victim of circumstance; who he is, is inseparable from his social and political duty. Deviation from that duty, no matter what might be the cause, must undermine his essential identity. In line with this, Bolingbroke, a fervent believer in social inequality, interpreted stockjobbing, public credit, political patronage, and factional competition as symptoms of a spiritual failure, a loss of moral personality. To his compatriots he said, in effect, "We seem to have forgotten who we are."

> Far from having the virtues, we have not even of vices, of great men. He who had pride instead of vanity, and ambition but equal to his desire of wealth, could never bear, I do not say, to be the understrapper to any farmer of royal authority, but to see patiently one of them, at best his fellow, perhaps his inferior in every respect, lord it over him, and the rest of mankind, dissipating the wealth, and trampling on the liberties of his country with impunity. This could not happen if there was the least spirit among us. But there is none. What passes among us for ambition, is an odd mixture of avarice and vanity: the moderation we have seen practiced, is pusillanimity, and the philosophy that some men affect, is sloth. Hence it comes that corruption has spread, and prevails.[28]

The way new modes of economic interaction and new forms of economic competition had severed the traditional ties between property and political capacity could not be indicted, in Bolingbroke's final analysis, for the decay of British liberty. That the members of the nobility would permit Walpole to turn the court into a "sanctuary for pickpockets and an hospital for changelings," allow themselves to be drawn into the "dark, intricate, and wicked mystery of stockjobbing," and consent to "bear anything, say anything, justify anything," in the name of some narrow faction, emanated, first and foremost, from nefarious indifference to reason and responsibility. By refusing to admit that the "service of our country is no chimerical, but a real duty," the aristocracy had, in Bolingbroke's view, torn down every moral and material provision against anarchy and oppression with its own hands.

> Some nations have received the yoke of servitude with little or no struggle; but if ever it is to be imposed upon us, we must not only hold out our necks to receive it, we must help to put it on. Now, to be passive in such a case is shameful; but to be active is supreme and unexampled infamy. In order to become slaves, we of this nation must be beforehand what other people have been rendered by a long course of servitude; we must become the most corrupt, the most profligate, the most senseless, the most servile nation of wretches, that ever disgraced humanity: for a force sufficient to ravish liberty from us, such as a great standing army is in time of peace, cannot be continued unless we continue it; nor can the means necessary to steal liberty from us, be long enough employed with effect, unless we give sanction to their iniquity, and call good evil, and evil good.[29]

Of course, despite these dire warnings, Walpole's system led not to anarchy and tyranny, but, as we know, to the growth of political stability.[30] The constitution never crumbled; Gibraltar never tumbled; none of Bolingbroke's prognostications about the progress of corruption ever came to pass. Bolingbroke's response to his age nevertheless repays careful attention, not only because it provides a mirror image to Mandeville's work, but also because it serves as an apt introduction to Hume and Smith's interpretations of the political problems produced by commercialization. A confirmed believer in aristocratic rule, Bolingbroke could not imagine how society might survive and, in a certain sense, flourish in the absence of economically independent and, therefore, morally legitimate political authority. When Bolingbroke could no longer identify any plausible alternative to Walpole's system, when he conceded the servility of the aristocracy, he could only seek salvation in a miraculous monarch because he assumed, like any good aristocrat, that the moral corruption of the elite violated the natural order to such an extent that society could only be freed from its Babylonian captivity by nearly divine intervention.

When Hume and Smith confronted this problem, when they examined the moral stature of the aristocracy, and found themselves obliged to admit some degree of truth in Mandeville's thesis, they were also obliged to investigate what Bolingbroke could never fathom, specifically, if private vices are public benefits, and, if it is, therefore, impossible to find a moral basis for political authority in the unequal distribution of property, then what keeps society from falling apart? Smith and Hume, who were as disinclined as Bolingbroke to contemplate an end to inequality, witnessed the political ineptitude which seemed to characterize the Whig oligarchy, and proceeded to ask the first question that usually occurs to elitists when they encounter what appears to be disorder, which is, "Who is in charge here?" The creative answers Hume and Smith supplied to this question will be explored in upcoming chapters; here it is sufficient to observe that Walpole's Mandevillean method of government led later theorists not to reject, but to reiterate many of Bolingbroke's conclusions. What remained most disturbing about Walpole's administration was, consequently, not the defects of his system, but the fact of his success.

IV

Hume's Critique
of the Whig Supremacy

W ere you to go to a dinner and find yourself seated between Mandeville and Bolingbroke, discovering Hume on the opposite side of
your table would be a huge relief. Leaning forward to hear him
would not only forestall Bolingbroke's relentless remarks on depravity and deter Mandeville from nudging you every time he
thought of something funny, it would allow you to hearken to what might
well have been the most judicious approach to the cultural, economic,
and political tendencies of the eighteenth century. Hume's temperate response to his times, which faltered only on the issue of the national debt,
is perhaps most clearly expressed in his reflections on the "Character of
Sir Robert Walpole." In this "Trifle," as he called it, Hume declined to
adopt the extravagant pitch of the opposition and likewise refrained from
inordinate praise of Whig administration. Instead, after carefully weigh-
ing Walpole's virtues against his vices, Hume concluded that all of the
minister's many admirable qualities should not deter any patriot from
urging an end to his power.

Sir ROBERT WALPOLE, prime minister of GREAT BRITAIN, is a man of ability, not a genius; good-natured, not virtuous; constant, not magnanimous; moderate, not equitable. . . . His ministry has been more advantageous to his family than to the public, better for this age than for posterity, and more pernicious by bad precedents than by real grievances. During his time, trade has flourished, liberty declined, and learning gone to ruin. As I am a man, I love him; as I am a scholar, I hate him; as I am a BRITON, I calmly wish his fall. And were I a member of either house, I would give my vote for removing him from ST. JAMES'S; but should be glad to see him retire to HOUGHTON-HALL, to pass the remainder of his days in ease and pleasure.[1]

There are at least three aspects of this passage which make it particularly indicative of Hume's reaction to his time. First, in line with the willingness here expressed to admit the complexity of Walpole's achievement, Hume constantly tried to transcend not only the distinctions between Whig and Tory, but also the boundaries between Court and Country. His effort to distance himself from Country diatribes against political corruption without falling into synch with Court-ordered hymns to modern Whiggism stemmed from his conviction that zeal, rather than the actual practices of Walpole's government or the basic beliefs of the Opposition, presented the most immediate threat to political peace. Hume, more specifically, specialized in dispassion, not merely because he happened to be disposed in that direction, but because his philosophical skepticism made him acutely aware of the dangers of overwrought appeals to reason or conviction and caused him to distrust the alarming accusations each party aimed at its counterpart.

Second, in keeping with the serious reservations contained in this passage, Hume's impatience with Country zealotry never led him to minimize the damage Walpole had done to his country. Hume's estimation of the decay of learning during Walpole's administration was, very deliberately, far removed from Bolingbroke's proclamations on barbarity. Nevertheless, Hume was perfectly willing to admit a severe defect of nobility in the minister's regime. In Hume's view, Walpole's government was kinder to trade than to refinement, more conducive to commerce than to education, because it catered to the vulgar ambitions of the many, rather than cultivating esoteric genius at the margins of society.

It is more easy to account for the . . . progress of commerce in any kingdom, than for that of learning . . . Avarice, or the desire of gain, is an universal passion, which operates at all times, in all places, and upon all persons: But curiosity, or the love of knowledge, has a very limited influence, and requires, youth, leisure, education, genius, and example, to make it govern any person. You will never want booksellers, while there are buyers of books: But there may frequently be readers where there are no authors.[2]

Hume's observations on the relationship between the progress of commerce and the cultivation of learning might, as first glance, seem to contradict his general conception of commerce as a civilizing force. To resolve that apparent contradiction, it is necessary first to examine a third aspect of Hume's reflections on Walpole's legacy, that is, that liberty had suffered under his command.

THE CONSEQUENCES OF PUBLIC CREDIT

When Hume remarked that Walpole had sinned less against his peers and more against posterity, he was referring to the hazards inherent in relying on public credit to manage the national debt. Walpole's addiction to this system, which drove him to deal with day-to-day expenses by drinking great draughts from the "sacred" sinking fund, followed, according to Hume, from a general failure to see that any politician who had been supplied with such means of maladministration could not possibly withstand the temptation of abuse. "It would," Hume remarked, "scarcely be more imprudent to give a prodigal son a credit in every banker's shop in London, than to impower a statesman to draw bills, in this manner, upon posterity."[3] Though Hume did not suggest, in the manner of Bolingbroke, that Walpole's financial habits had carried the nation to the very edge of destruction, he insisted that the practice of robbing the future to maintain the present would, if it continued, undoubtedly lead to that result. "The abuses of mortgaging are . . . certain and inevitable: poverty, impotence, and subjection to foreign powers."[4]

There were several circumstances produced by public credit which caused Hume to issue this uncharacteristic ultimatum, including a rise in the cost of labor, a shortage of hard currency, and unhealthy levels of foreign investment. More than all of these, however, Hume emphasized the perils inherent in the ever increasing power and profligate inclinations of those who lived off the interest of the public debt. Parasites such as these fed from the public trough, but maintained no real bond with the public; their invisible, unreliable, and unaccountable resources might be dispatched at any time to any country, dissolved without any public notice, or dissipated in anonymous excess in any great city. But if the debt continued to rise, taxes on land would have to rise with it and, once the landholders—the owners of fixed, socially determinate, and politically rooted assets—had been bled dry, the stockholders would retain whatever wealth might remain in an otherwise destitute society. Since, as Adam Smith wrote in another connection, the revenue of the stockholders "costs them neither labour nor care, but comes to them, as it were, of its own accord,"[5] these men would, according to Hume, "sink into the lethargy of a stupid and pampered luxury, without spirit, ambition, or enjoyment."[6]

Against those who tried to pretend that the transfer of wealth through taxes and credit merely moved property from person to person, without impinging on national prosperity, Hume insisted that, while it might not much disturb the public if, with the passing of time, the descendants of those who rode "in the coaches" ended up as servants sitting "upon the boxes," such a transformation would knock down the obvious distinctions between the "idle and laborious" segments of society and, thereby, subvert the natural connections between property and power. The assets passed from one generation to the next in such an "unnatural state," would consist only in stocks, which, Hume wrote, "convey no hereditary authority or credit to the possessor." With the dissolution of this natural authority, and the destruction of "all ideas of nobility, gentry, and family," so would go every defense against absolute tyranny. Liberated from the influence of an autonomous aristocracy, the sovereign would gain complete ascendancy. Under these conditions, Hume declared,

> The several ranks of men, which form a kind of independent magistracy in a state, instituted by the hand of nature, are entirely lost; and every man of authority derives his influence from the commission alone of the sovereign. No expedient remains for . . . suppressing insurrections, but mercenary armies: No expedient at all remains for resisting tyranny: Elections are swayed by bribery and corruption alone: and the middle power between the king and his people being totally removed, a grievous despotism must infallibly prevail. The

landholders, despised for their poverty, and hated for their oppressions, will be utterly unable to make any opposition to it.[7]

Having set forth this appalling prospect, Hume did not suggest that much might be done to avoid it. In fact, he not only concluded that this was the "situation to which Great Britain [was] visibly tending," he remarked that people are, for the most part, such "great dupes," that national bankruptcy would probably be insufficient to avert a resuscitation of the whole ruinous system, until the growth of the funds had so exhausted every natural resource that the nation would almost willingly surrender to foreign invasion.[8]

Though his condemnation of public credit echoes many of Bolingbroke's complaints about Walpole's administration, Hume did not fall into the trap set in the *Fable of the Bees*. In contrast to Bolingbroke, who pushed his criticism of commercial development so far that he seemed to recommend unbearable austerity, Hume celebrated the social, cultural, and moral benefits of commercial progress. "Ages of refinement," are, he declared, "both the happiest and the most virtuous." Thanks to the expansion of domestic industry and foreign trade, the members of society become increasingly active, inquisitive and sociable. They come together in cities, meet in business and social circles and, as a consequence of this social interaction, develop more delicate tastes, more elegant manners, and more satisfying and elaborate forms of social exchange. From all of this, Hume inferred,

> They must feel an increase of humanity, from the very habit of convening together, and contributing to each other's pleasures and entertainment. Thus, industry, knowledge and humanity are linked together, by an indissoluble chain, and are found, from experience as well as reason, to be peculiar to the more polished, and what are commonly denominated, the more luxurious ages.[9]

Against the Country party's preoccupation with the moral and political superiority of ancient republics, Hume took the Court Whig position that the social and economic structure of modern society is far more consistent with our natural inclinations. His argument with those who preached against luxury and corruption (which sounds a lot like Mandeville might have had he ever stopped kidding) was not that their morals were severely mistaken, but that they advocated an unnatural system of social and political discipline, a system which they themselves would never actually follow, since it would require them to take the hard road traveled by Mandeville's bees.

> Could we convert a city into a kind of fortified camp and infuse into each breast so martial a genius and such a passion for public good as to make everyone willing to undergo the greatest hardships for the sake of the public, these affections might now, as in ancient times, prove alone a sufficient spur to industry and support the community. It would then be advantageous, as in camps, to banish all arts and luxury. . . . But as these principles are too disinterested and too difficult to support, it is requisite to govern men by other passions and animate them with a spirit of avarice and industry, art and luxury. . . . The harmony of the whole is still supported, and the natural bent of the mind being more complied with, individuals as well as the public find their account in the observance of these maxims.[10]

Some scholars have interpreted Hume's appreciation of the natural advantages of commercial society as an effort to overcome every moral and political problem posed by the universal pursuit of private gain. There is, however, no reason to suppose that Hume ever imagined that it might be his job to clear up such problems, however much historians might desire him to take up that task. If so much scholarship on the history of ideas did not proceed from the premise that every major historical development must be either preceded or accompanied by a philosophical rationale, this obvious point would be entirely unnecessary. However, recent studies of eighteenth-century Anglo-American political philosophy have suffered sorely from the unspoken but determinative assumption that we might never have seen the rise of capitalism or, for that matter, the formulation of the U.S. Constitution, if Hume or Adam Smith had not found some way to overcome the classical republican critique of commercialization. But Hume did not supply commercial development with any sort of philosophical salvation, nor did he play the role of John the Baptist in relation to Adam Smith.[11] Instead, as a moral philosopher rather than a problem solver he felt it was his duty to define the dilemmas produced by the interaction between history and human nature and to articulate how our natural inclinations, both good and bad, manifest themselves in commercial change.

POLITICS AND THE PRIMACY OF PASSION

With this in mind, Hume's trepidation about certain facets of Walpole's administration falls into line with his analysis of the natural evolution of political institutions which falls, in turn, into line with his preoccupation with the primacy of passion over reason and, particularly, with the primacy of the passion for personal gain. The unifying factor in all of these aspects of Hume's philosophy is that all were developed to show that the pursuit of private interest simultaneously serves as the key to social and political development and as the most powerful and pernicious threat to social and political order. Of all of the passions, Hume asserted,

> This avidity alone of *acquiring* goods and possessions for ourselves and our nearest friends is insatiable, perpetual, universal, and directly destructive of society. There is scarce anyone who is not actuated by it; and there is no one who has not reason to fear from it when it acts without restraint and gives way to its first and most natural movements. So that, upon the whole, we are to esteem the difficulties in the establishment of society to be greater or less according to those we encounter in regulating and restraining this passion.[12]

In order to check the "natural movements" of this all-consuming passion, human beings must submit to collective rules of conduct which force them, no matter how indisposed they might otherwise be, "to consult their real and permanent interests," and, as a result, distinguish their own possessions from those of other people. Fortunately, Hume argued, the evolution of these rules did not require any appeal to reason or depend on the adoption of some original compact. Instead, the members of society arrived at the convention which permits stability of possession the moment that relative scarcity collided with limitless desire; in the absence of absolute abundance, universal license taught that self-interest can only find fulfillment in social control. This lesson, which, along with the distinctions between justice and injustice, inspired our essential ideas of "*property, right, and obligation,*" arose from the most fundamental forms of social exchange. There is, therefore, no reason to resort to the philosophical fiction of the state of nature to explain the origins of society and the establishment of justice. The personal advantages conferred by such social constraints are, Hume argued, so plainly apparent that the convention that secures stability of possession must have coincided with the very beginnings of social life.

> Now as it is by establishing the rule for the stability of possession that [the love of gain] restrains itself, if that rule be very abstruse and of very difficult of invention, society must be deemed in a manner accidental and the effect of many ages. But if it be found that nothing can be more simple and obvious than that rule that every parent, in order to preserve peace among his children, must establish it, and that these first rudiments of justice must every day be improved as society enlarges . . . we may conclude that it is utterly impossible for men to remain any considerable time in that savage condition which precedes society, but that his very first state and situation may justly be deemed social.

Given the role of the passion for personal gain in the origins of society, one could, according to Hume, draw the conclusions reached by writers such as Mandeville and insist that social relations arise from the viciousness of human nature. In the final analysis, however, these conclusions fail to clarify the actual facts of the matter; to talk about vice and virtue with regard to the natural evolution of society is to confuse moral judgment with philosophical comprehension of the topic at hand.

> The question, therefore, concerning the wickedness or goodness of human nature enters not the least into that other question concerning the origin of society; nor is there anything to be considered but the degree of men's sagacity or folly. For whether the passion of self-interest be esteemed vicious or virtuous, it is all a case, since it alone restrains it; so that if it be virtuous, men become social by their virtue; if vicious, their vice has the same effect.[13]

As usual, Hume's point was that moral distinctions are irrelevant to our understanding of the realities of nature. That selfishness and other moral defects so fundamentally determine the conditions our existence might be grounds for regret, but that regret plays or ought to play no part in discussions which are designed to delineate the natural and unalterable principles of human conduct. Hume was, in this sense, prepared to admit that there was some irony in deriving positive effects from negative inclinations, but, against Mandeville, he refused to regard it as a real paradox.

In his account of the evolution of government, Hume adopted a similarly detached approach to double-edged effects of the pursuit of private advantage. Self-interest, he argued, may make us conscious of the necessity of justice, but it is also the very force which constantly inclines us to violate its rules. Moreover, in line with the natural confines of our reason and affections, it generally inclines us to do so for the most vulgar and obvious reasons.

> All men are sensible of the necessity of justice to maintain peace and order, and all men are sensible of the necessity of peace and justice for the maintenance of society. Yet notwithstanding this strong and obvious necessity—such is the frailty or perverseness of our nature!—it is impossible to keep men faithfully and unerringly in the paths of justice. Some extraordinary circumstances may happen in which a man finds his interests to be more promoted by fraud and repine than hurt by the breach which his injustice makes in the social union. But much more frequently he is seduced from his great and important, but distant interests by the allurement of present, though often very frivolous temptations. This great weakness is incurable in human nature.[14]

Because self-interest constantly leads us into temptation, blinding us both to our duty to others and to our own genuine needs, we must turn to government to add compulsion to conscience: "In a word, obedience is a new duty which must be invented to support that of justice." But the prompting of personal interest, Hume characteristically observed, not only makes government necessary, it dictates the manner in which political authority gradually establishes itself. "Love of dominion" originally encourages some superior individual to set himself up as the leader of society; and, having assumed that position, he finds that the best way to consolidate his personal power is to administer justice in an impartial way. To achieve this end, he soon "establishes subordinate ministers and often a military force, who find an immediate and visible interest in supporting his authority."[15] Over time, as the rule of justice evolves into a regular feature of everyday life, the members of society gradually begin to support government not so much out of fear as habit; inured to obedience, they "never think of departing from that path in which they and their ancestors have constantly trod and to which they are confined by so many urgent and visible motives."[16]

Hume's explanation of the evolution of government was obviously intended to expose the utopian expectations of social contract theory. While admitting that government might have been originally founded on consent, he stressed that the members of society lack the wisdom and foresight required to understand the need to maintain effective political authority. In fact, he argued, if human beings were ever so committed to justice that they would freely and consistently consent to make the "great sacrifice of liberty [which] must necessarily be made in every government," government itself would be rendered unnecessary: "Were all men possessed of so inflexible a regard to justice that of themselves they would totally abstain from the properties of others, they had forever remained in a state of absolute liberty, without subjection to any magistrate or political society." Likewise, if the members of society were able to reflect on their own genuine interests and, on the basis of that reflection, managed to establish a contract between the rulers and the ruled, conquest and usurpation would have no place in political history: "Again, were all men possessed of so perfect an understanding as always to understand their own interests, no form of government had been submitted to but what was founded on consent and was fully canvassed by every member of the society. But this state of perfection is likewise much superior to human nature."[17]

We have only, Hume argued, to glance around the globe to see that social contract theory is about as far removed from reality as the poetic dream of the golden age. Not only is it impossible to discover any government which even pretends to founded upon a compact made between the rulers and the ruled, but everywhere we find rulers who, having risen to power by the use of brute force, demand obedience from subjects who have not the vaguest conception of voluntary consent. The people, far from exacting promises from government, are generally made to submit to its dictates first by the threat of immediate punishment and then by the unquestioning force of habit and custom.

The Revolution of 1688, which the Whigs attempted to justify as a restoration of the original compact between the people and their rulers, presents itself as a crucial case in point. In the first place, it was only the royal succession which was then affected, and it was only the political elite who decided the fate of the whole country. Though the people went along with that decision, Hume observed, they played absolutely no role in the alteration of the state: "But was the matter left in the least to their choice? Was it not justly supposed to be from that moment decided and every man punished who refused to submit to the new sovereign? How otherwise could the matter have ever been brought to any issue or conclusion?" Thus, even the Glorious Revolution, which secured "the most entire system of liberty that was ever known amongst mankind," contradicted the purely "speculative principle" of rational and voluntary consent.[18]

For Hume, the problem with social contract theory was the same problem that undermined classical republican critiques of commercial progress: both failed to take account of the natural limitations that determine the structure of society and the strength of political order. On one hand, by overestimating the reach of reason, social contract theorists inspired the dangerous and destabilizing idea that government requires popular consent. On the other, by preaching up moral transformation, Bolingbroke and his circle fomented faction and cultivated an unhealthy zeal for political change. Against these enthusiastic claims, and in keeping with his conviction that government can only be sustained by custom, habit, and tradition, Hume endlessly stressed the importance of putting what is before what ought to be.

Hume's conclusions about the role of corruption in the preservation of the British constitution conform precisely to this spirit of philosophical moderation. Against opposition writers like Bolingbroke, Hume took the Mandevillean position that government must be designed to accommodate the irrational ambitions of the majority of society. In keeping with his conviction that human beings are inclined, first and foremost, to seek their own advantage, he agreed with the conclusions of those political theorists who

> have established it as a maxim that, in contriving any system of government, and fixing the several checks and controls of the constitution, every man ought to be supposed a knave, and to have no other end, in all his actions, than private interest. By this interest we must govern him, and by means of it, make him, notwithstanding his insatiable avarice and ambition, co-operate to the public good. Without this, say they, we shall in vain boast of all the advantages of any constitution, and shall find, in the end, that we have no security in our liberties and possessions, except the good-will of our rulers; that is, we shall have no security at all.[19]

Given that the fundamental function of an effective constitution is to make it "the interest, even of bad men, to act for the public good," Hume emphasized that those in power should always be "restrained by the most rigid laws," so as to make it "easy to discover either the good or bad intentions of a minister and to judge whether his personal character deserve love or hatred." After all, he pointed out, "in the smallest court or office, the stated forms and methods by which business must be conducted are found to be a considerable check upon the natural depravity of mankind. Why should not the case be the same in public affairs?"[20]

In light of the peculiar balance of powers within Britain's own "mixed government," Hume argued that those in office had to be held in check, not only by the threat of punishment, but also by the promise of reward. The power of the Crown, which had been diminished both by restrictions imposed in the Revolution settlement and by a general loss of respect for authority, could not hope to hold its own against the power of the Commons unless the king enjoyed the resources necessary to dispense political patronage, that is, unless he and his ministers had at their disposal revenue sufficient to offer positions, pensions and various preferments to the members of parliament. Fortunately, Hume observed,

> In our present constitution, many accidents which have rendered governments every where, as well as in Great Britain, much more burdensome than formerly, have thrown into the hands of the crown the disposal of a large revenue, and have enabled the king, by the private interest and ambition of the members, to restrain the public interest and ambition of the body. While the opposition . . . endeavors to draw every branch of government under the cognizance of parliament, the courtiers reserve a part to the disposal of the crown; and the royal prerogative, though deprived of its ancient powers, still maintains a due weight in the balance of the constitution.

The concentration of property and political power within the Commons, along with the fact that its members were naturally driven by private interest, made the system of royal influence, which the Country party constantly condemned as the greatest threat to British liberty, and which even the supporters of the Court found difficult to publicly defend, an inescapable feature of the modern regime: "We may, therefore, give to this influence what name we please; we may call it by the invidious appellations of corruption and dependence, but some degree and some kind of it are inseparable from the very nature of the constitution."[21]

Hume's arguments in favor of corruption, along with his preference for modern over ancient societies, might seem to indicate that he was closer to the Court than to the Country party. Indeed, against Boling-broke, one of those "TORIES," who had been so long "obliged to talking in the republican stile, that they seem[ed] to have made converts of themselves by their hypocrisy, " Hume pointed out that, if Walpole had really been able to drive the nation to such depths of perfidy, then the constitution so revered by all patriots would hardly be worthy of such lavish praise.[22]

> If our constitution be really that noble fabric, the pride of Britain, the envy of our neighbors, raised by the labor of so many centuries, repaired at the expense of so many millions, and cemented by such a profusion of blood—I say, if our constitution does in any degree deserve these eulogies, it would never have suffered a weak and wicked minister to govern triumphantly for the course of twenty years when opposed by the greatest geniuses in the nation, who exercised the utmost liberty of tongue and pen in Parliament, and in their frequent appeals to the people. But if the minister be wicked and weak to the degree so strenuously insisted on, the constitution must be faulty in its original principles, and he cannot consistently be charged with undermining the best form of government in the world.[23]

As keen as he might have been the contradictions within Country ideology, Hume did not reject it out of hand. He agreed, for example, at least until late in his life, with the Country party's arguments for a citizen's militia and against a large standing army. Moreover, for all of his praise of refinement, and despite his own concessions to parliamentary corruption, he ultimately accepted the central argument of the opposition and acknowledged that the overgrowth of royal power, combined with the decline of public morality, would, in the end, undermine the constitutional foundations of British liberty. In his essay, "Whether the British Government Inclines More to Absolute Monarchy, or to a Republic," Hume contrasted the "specious" reasoning of those who forecast the advent of popular government with the overdrawn but plausible conclusions of those who called attention to the constant efforts of the crown to enlarge its civil and military capacity. Hume was, of course, careful not to toss off any impolitic assertions, but he tilted, without too much qualification, toward the position that the expansion of royal prerogative presented the most immediate threat.

> When we add to [the monarch's] great property, the increasing luxury of the nation, our proneness to corruption, together with the great power and prerogatives of the crown, and the command of military force, there is no one but must despair of being able, without extraordinary efforts, to support our free government much longer under these disadvantages.[24]

To Hume, the forces at work in British history presented two unfortunate alternatives. On one hand, the present state of affairs might degenerate into a turbulent and violent republic which would soon be transformed into absolute tyranny; on the other, Britain might avoid this terrible prospect and preserve social order by calmly and deliberately establishing absolute government straight away. In view of the priority of authority over liberty in the preservation of civil society, Hume chose the relative safety of despotic power: "Absolute monarchy, therefore, is the easiest death, the true Euthanasia of the British constitution."[25]

Hume's unflinching commentary on the fate of the constitution—to paraphrase the conclusion to his essay "Of the Original Contract"—built a Country consequence of constitutional corruption on a Court foundation of commercial progress.[26] Like Mandeville and the Court Whigs, Hume wasted no time lamenting the loss of ancient virtue and republican independence in the course of commercial development; at the same time, however, he shared Bolingbroke's trepidation about the decay of aristocratic authority within the new commercial order. The method he chose to put an end to British liberty derived from his conviction that, no matter what dangers lurked in the growth of royal prerogative, there was far more to fear from popular government because a society without any fixed hierarchy, and which failed to adhere to established customs and traditions, could not inculcate submission to political institutions without resorting to violence.

THE IMAGE OF AUTHORITY IN COMMERCIAL SOCIETY

This exploration of Hume's response to the Whig supremacy is not by any means designed to provide a full account of his philosophical perspective. However, to appreciate the depth of his dread of popular government, it helps to acknowledge how far his notions of established social hierarchy entered into the basic principles of his moral philosophy. In the chapter on "Liberty and Necessity" in his *Treatise on Human Nature*, for example, one of the most dramatic examples he used to demonstrate the uniformity of the natural rules of behavior was the division of society into various ranks. It is, he argued, this natural division which not only inspires every species of industry and invention, but which determines the essential qualities and conditions of human experience.

> The skin, pores, muscles, and nerves of a day-labourer are different from those of a man of quality; so are his sentiments, actions, and manners. The different stations of life influence the whole fabric, external and internal; and these different stations arise necessarily because uniformly, from the necessary and uniform principles of human nature. Men cannot live without society and cannot be associated without government. Government establishes the different ranks of men. This produces industry, traffic, manufactures, lawsuits, war, leagues, alliances, voyages, travels, cities, fleets, ports, and all those other actions and objects which cause such a diversity, and at the same time maintain such an uniformity in human life.[27]

Hume, of course, never suggested that commercial development would somehow obliterate all of these natural social distinctions, but he did fear that the transfer and transformation of property under Walpole's government would render the boundaries between the various stations invisible and, consequently, drive a wedge between social hierarchy and political control. By confusing the palpable differences between those who ride "in the coaches" and those who sit "upon the boxes," and thereby destroying the proper and accepted proportion between the few and the many, the radical alteration of property relations caused by public credit would, in Hume's view, choke "use and practice," the only means available to assert "authority and precedent," the natural fountains of political security and peace.[28] The crux of Hume's case against Walpole was, consequently, not what Bolingbroke found so ghastly—that he governed by corruption—but that his system unhinged property relations from entrenched beliefs about social identity, political duty, and compliance with what might be described as the customary chain of social and political command.

In an ironic way (and it would, of course, be insulting tradition not to stress irony here), Hume's pragmatic approach to politics led him to conclusions that were if not meaningless then at least directionless in relation to the positions taken by Mandeville and Bolingbroke. When Mandeville reflected on the moral ambiguities of his society, he managed to make the hypocrisy he perceived not merely more tolerable but positively entertaining by reducing what he saw to a steady stream of jokes. Bolingbroke, on the other hand, found some relief from the apparent decline of moral and political standards in the idea that pervasive corruption might be corrected either by future generations or by the admittedly unlikely emergence of a patriot king. But Hume, who lacked Mandeville's merciless sense of humor, consistently rejected Bolingbroke's speculative ideas about moral reformation and political rebirth. Confronted with increasing economic interdependence, decreasing regard for the majesty of the crown, and vanishing respect for established ideas of nobility, gentry, and family, Hume's lack of faith in the power of reason, as well as his antipathy towards any significant intervention in the natural course of things, left him no road to follow save for the "featureless path of calm resignation."[29] Having seated social hierarchy and political ascendancy on the uncertain pillar of public opinion, Hume not only reduced the defects of political authority to a problem of image only, he ended up having to argue against the very idea of change. "The spirit of innovation is," he declared, "in itself pernicious, howsoever favourable its particular object may sometimes appear."[30]

Given the weakness inherent in this degree of conservatism, it is easy to see why Hume took the line of least resistance to absolute power. The significance he gave to socially ingrained, culturally entrenched, politically indisputable habits of obedience disposed him to recommend political moderation not merely as a brake on tumult and disorder but as the best way to encourage unthinking submission to established authority.

> Moderation is of advantage to every establishment: Nothing but zeal can overturn a settled power: An over-active zeal in friends is apt to beget a like spirit in antagonists. The transition from moderate opposition against an establishment, to an entire acquiescence in it, is easy and insensible.[31]

Since he had pinned his hopes on the dubious supposition that zeal might give way to moderation which, in turn, might evolve into unreflective conformity, it is hardly surprising that, once in a while, Hume's philo-sophical temper became a little frayed. In his essay "Of the Coalition of Parties," for example, his attempt to silence loose talk about ancient lib-erty and popular consent sounds less like the arguments of a philosopher and more like the impatient admonitions of a harried aristocrat.

> But the people must not pretend, because they can, by their consent, lay the foundations of government, that therefore they are permit-ted, at their pleasure, to overthrow and subvert them. There is no end of these seditious and arrogant claims. The power of the crown is now openly struck at: the nobility are also in visible peril: The gentry will soon follow: The popular leaders, who will then assume the name of gentry, will next be exposed to danger. And the people themselves, having become incapable of civil government, and lying under the restraint of no authority, must, for the sake of peace, admit, instead of their legal and mild monarchs, a succession of military and despotic tyrants.[32]

Though Hume's consternation about the deterioration of deference to authority has been chalked up to a late conversion to Tory pessimism, it seems unhelpful to force his philosophical politics into such a narrow frame.[33] Throughout his career, Hume not only drew whatever sense he could from both the Court and Country parties, he spurned, along with the "clamor" of the Whigs, the "old prejudices" of the Tories.[34] If he leaned in the direction of the last and understood why they "defied" Whig oligarchy, it seems more accurate to describe that bias as the logical outgrowth of his skeptical approach to government than to reduce it to partisanship.[35]

In fact, Hume's refusal to involve himself in party conflict and fac-tional division helps to explain the ultimate lack of substance in his politi-cal convictions and, at long last, introduces the apolitical approach to history and society adopted by his friend, Adam Smith. Hume would not identify himself as Whig or Tory or define his principles as Court or Country because these labels appeared to require either exaggerated faith in the power of reason or immoderate expectations of moral reform. Hume, who anchored political possibility in ordinary experience, never supposed that Whig oligarchy operated according to any conceivable stan-dard of rationality, nor did he imagine that a change of government might erase the imperfections of human nature which were so apparent in the way ministers, monarchs, and politicians managed their affairs. Instead, having reduced politics to an arena for the pursuit of private advantage, he accepted government as an expression of our natural limitations and, in so doing, removed what Adam Smith called the "study of wisdom and the practice of virtue" from the political sphere (*TMS*, 61). The most individuals can extract from political participation, in this context, is not, as Bolingbroke would have it, to achieve the worthiest goals and conform to the highest ideals, but to reach, in "an easy and insensible" way, "an entire acquiescence" to orthodox practice and prevailing conditions.

Without suggesting that Hume was a superficial thinker, his essays make it plain that his political standpoint was superficial to the extent that his conception of the primacy of the passion for personal gain deprived political conduct of what had been seen, not only by republicans, but throughout the history of political philosophy, as its moral dimension, that is, the conviction that the members of society realize themselves as rational and fully human beings when they deliberate as autonomous citizens. The foundation of this autonomy, as set forth by Aristotle and upheld until the emergence of commercial modernity, was the protection from corruption conferred by property ownership. Thus, when Hume defined the "avidity of acquiring goods" as "perpetual and universal" and stressed that the principles of human nature are everywhere the same, he also gave up the notion that political authority must be legitimized by moral superiority. In Hume's world, the propertied minority is subject to the same imperfections that determine the behavior of the propertyless majority. Consequently, Hume's response to the basic question of political philosophy, Who should rule? was, more or less, Whoever happens to be in charge. Hume's measure of authority was, more precisely, not rationality or morality (or any other yardstick of desert) but functionality; in line with the role he assigned to habit and tradition, he judged government according to its capacity to inculcate obedience by sustaining an appearance of control.

If Hume looked at the Whig oligarchy and, after careful study of history and philosophy, decided that self-interest must be the animating principle of government and society, Smith concluded from the same example that it would be ridiculous to suppose that the machinations of narrow-minded grandees, ministers, kings, and politicians might control the fate of the world. Like Hume, Smith could not help but notice that, for all of Mandeville's jokes about moral degradation or Bolingbroke's grave announcements about luxury and corruption, the self-interested pursuits of the British aristocracy did not impinge on national prosperity; in fact, society seemed to flourish however much they neglected their ostensible duty to promote the public welfare.

In contrast to Hume, however, who called on the aristocracy to maintain at least the appearance of superiority, Smith concluded that those who pretended to rule society ought to concede their own incompetence and quit interfering in other people's affairs. Smith, the subject of Chapter 5, agreed with much of what Mandeville and Bolingbroke had to say about the corruption and degeneracy of the British aristocracy. But from that corruption and degeneracy, he deduced not that society would disintegrate if they failed to mend their ways, as Bolingbroke had argued, or that they might not command a proper degree of deference, as Hume had warned, but that their political incapacity was, for the most part, irrelevant to the preservation and prosperity of humanity. Chapter 5 is accordingly designed to show how the eighteenth-century critique of aristocratic depravity culminated in Smith's vehement defense of free enterprise.

V

Adam Smith and
the End of Aristocracy

Though it might be an exaggeration to tag Adam Smith as the most influential theorist who ever lived, he would place high in a free competition. What makes his pivotal role in Western philosophy particularly striking is that his status can be ascribed, at least in part, to "constant," "uniform," and, since the nineteenth century, "uninterrupted" confusion about his contribution to political thought. Marx, whose own reputation has lately fallen into disarray, could be implicated in this misunderstanding, but rather than waste time trying to remove a splinter from his eye, it makes more sense to clear away some of the planks which continue to block our vision.[1]

First among these is the notion that Smith was destined to invent some sort of alibi for the rise of capitalism. Against this, certain Smith scholars might protest, "You are living in the past!" We have so far abandoned the word "capitalism" that we are beginning to doubt that such a system ever existed. We have, moreover, not only left off talking about Smith as an apologist for the bourgeoisie, if that class ever appeared on this planet, we found out that Smith's philosophy is immeasurably more complex than any Marxist ever imagined. In the interstices of the *Theory of Moral Sentiments* and the intricacies of the *Wealth of Nations*, we have discovered, among other things, that Smith was an advocate of agrarian rather than industrial capitalism; that his political economy ought to be viewed not as an introduction to the "dismal science" of the nineteenth century, but as an effort to defend the British aristocracy against classical republican critics of commercial modernity; that he tried to promote civic virtue, if not for the commercial world at large, then at least for the young men of Scotland; and that he dealt with the moral defects of commercial activity by placing his arguments within a jurisprudential framework which, if he had not died before he had a chance to explain it, surely would have allowed everything he wrote to make a lot more sense.[2]

This caricature of recent Smith scholarship is not designed to dispute the indisputable insights each of these interpretations provides. The point here is that these studies all proceed from the premise that Smith's work must have had some exculpatory purpose, so that if he is no longer viewed as a vindicator of nineteenth-century capitalism, he is still described as an advocate for the socioeconomic system from which, like it or not, capitalist society probably evolved. Smith scholars have, in other words, yet to relinquish the notion that Smith felt obliged to apologize for something, though that something may not have been the exploitative methods of a rising middle class.

The alternative assumption offered here is that, rather than defending any particular social or political system, or trying to justify any particular mode of behavior, Smith's overarching purpose was to show that society is held together not by any moral code, not by any political scheme, but by the very defects that prevent us from behaving in a morally correct and politically competent manner. More specifically, by identifying the natural pursuit of self-interest as both the ruling principle of individual conduct and the foundation of social development, Smith was trying to show that judgments about what is morally acceptable or what is politically desirable are irrelevant to the natural course of progress and the inevitable spread of prosperity.

Smith was, in other words, not attempting to resolve any moral or political dilemma. On the contrary, his plainly painful thesis was that moral corruption and political incompetence are unavoidable aspects of social development. The *Theory of Moral Sentiments* and the *Wealth of Nations* can consequently be accurately described, as has lately been argued, as answers to critique of commerce contained in classical republican philosophy, but rather than furnishing philosophical weapons against moral decay and political incapacity, both works offer full and complete surrender.[3] To march this somewhat distasteful metaphor one step farther, Smith's response to the classical republican attack on commerce as a threat to political virtue was not to find some strategy to rescue politics from corruption, but to advise all combatants to withdraw from the field.

In case the fact that Smith offered political advice might seem to imply that he advocated particular policies, it should be emphasized that, while it may be said that he was trying to instruct ministers, kings, and politicians on their own grave limitations, he had not much hope that his admonitions would be gladly received. His case against mercantilism was, after all, that political leaders lack even the small degree of sense that Mandeville was willing to allow them. But if the downside of Smith's conclusions about the infirmities that plague those who pretend to rule society was that those rulers would be unlikely to heed his counsel, the upside was that, in most cases, their incapacities are insufficient to obstruct the natural course of economic progress.

> The uniform, constant, and uninterrupted effort of every man to better his condition, the principle from which publick and national, as well as private opulence is originally derived, is frequently powerful enough to maintain the natural progress of things toward improvement, in spite both of the extravagance of government, and the greatest errors of administration. Like the unknown principle of animal life, it frequently restores health and vigor to the constitution, in spite, not only of the disease, but of the absurd prescriptions of the doctor.[4]

In light of this typical example of Smith's disposition toward government, it is clear that anyone who chooses to read his work as a vindication of commercial aristocracy must admit that the strategy he adopted to defend his clients was, first, to establish their mental incompetence and, second, to show that their very real transgressions might be reduced to misdemeanors in the universal scheme.

Though Smith's theory of economic development was more than a generalization from the vicissitudes of Whig oligarchy, it is fair to say that his reaction to the rise of commercial aristocracy, to what Mandeville had reduced to moral hypocrisy, to what Bolingbroke had denounced as an inherently unstable form of society, to what Hume had seen as a prelude to absolute monarchy, was to say good-bye to aristocratic ideas of nobility, gentry, and family as fundamental principles of social cohesion. In short, Smith concluded that the probity of the ruling elite, which had been thought to be essential to maintain the political and material structure of society, made very little difference to the steady spread of prosperity through all of the various ranks within the social whole. In contrast to Mandeville, Bolingbroke, and Hume, not to mention the mainstream of previous political thinkers, Smith surmised that society could withstand the corruption of those at the top because, no matter what they themselves believe, they are simply not in charge of social order.

The shortest way to describe Smith's response to commercial development is to say that he rejected the concept of aristocratic government, but never stopped thinking like an aristocrat. Along with Mandeville, Bolingbroke, and Hume, Smith continued to regard the pursuit of economic self-interest as a morally corrupting threat to individual autonomy; unlike these predecessors, however, he not only accepted the pursuit of private advantage as the mainstay of society, he argued that the rule of self-interest makes political virtue both impossible and unnecessary. Smith's doctrine of unintended consequences was thus designed to illustrate two basic principles: first, that the passion for personal gain naturally governs human behavior and, second, that, however much this corrupting passion might incapacitate individuals, however much it might prevent them from knowing, willing, or understanding the real results of their actions, it automatically fosters economic growth. By pointing out the positive effects of the uninterrupted pursuit of personal advantage, Smith was not trying to supply self-regard with a novel degree of rationality or transform it into a new way to exercise individual autonomy. He was trying to illustrate that this irrational desire animates every member of society, high as well as low, and, therefore, makes it impossible to draw any meaningful moral distinctions between the lowliest laborer and the loftiest grandee.

THE UNREALITY OF THE SOCIAL ELITE

Throughout the *Theory of Moral Sentiments*, Smith cited the pursuit of personal wealth and power not only as the key to social prosperity, but also as evidence against the pretension that social status indicates genuine superiority. Our highest ambition is, he maintained, to merit and to obtain the respect and esteem of our fellow human beings. We are, upon coming into the world, confronted with two very different paths to these ends: we can follow the example of those who study wisdom and practice virtue or we can model ourselves after those who possess wealth and social position. The example of the former, though it is "more correct and more exquisitely beautiful," is unfortunately eclipsed by that of the latter, which is "more gaudy and glittering." It is, consequently, obvious which of these is the road less traveled by.

> They are the wise and the virtuous chiefly, a select, though I am afraid, but a small party, who are the real and steady admirers of wisdom and virtue. The great mob of mankind are the admirers and worshippers . . . of wealth and greatness. . . . It is scarce agreeable to good morals or even to good language, perhaps, to say that wealth and greatness, abstracted from merit and virtue, deserve our respect. We must acknowledge, however, that they almost constantly obtain it, and that they may therefore be considered as, in some respects, the natural objects of it. (*TMS*, 63)

Note that Smith has here transformed the traditional philosophical vision of society as a layered pyramid. The wise and virtuous few, those who had been, at least in the realm of political philosophy, supposed to occupy the summit of society, have been pushed aside. The possessors of wealth and greatness, those who stand at the pinnacle in this picture, maintain their exalted positions not because they deserve to do so, but because the mob has mistakenly raised them to the top of the social scale. Here, in stark contrast to Bolingbroke, who assumed that social stratification proceeds from basic moral principles, and also in contrast to Hume, who assumed that social hierarchy is sustained, if not by any appeal to reason, then at least by time-honored customs and beliefs, Smith attributed the natural divisions within society to popular fantasies about the possession of wealth and power.

For Smith, the fact that these fantasies are natural and inevitable did not make them any less morally objectionable. Smith's vision of social order thus "out-Humed" Hume's assertion that the world is ruled by opinion; according to Smith, the world is ruled not by habit and tradition; but by morally disagreeable illusions. In line with this relatively radical degree of skepticism, Smith went out of his way to emphasize the morally corrupting aspects of our natural inclination to pay homage to those who seem to ride high in the social firmament.

> This disposition to admire, and almost to worship, the rich and the powerful, and to despise, or at least to neglect, persons of poor and mean condition, though necessary both to establish and to maintain the distinction of ranks and the order of society, is, at the same time, the great and most universal cause of the corruption of our moral sentiments. (*TMS*, 61)

Likewise, in a manner which was sometimes remarkably severe, he insisted that the natural desire for personal fortune is entirely mistaken and, in those few cases in which it is actually fulfilled, finally disappointing. The passion for wealth and power is, he observed,

> seldom consistent with perfect tranquillity, the foundation of all real and satisfactory enjoyment. Neither is it always certain that, in the splendid situation we aim at, those real and satisfactory pleasures can be enjoyed with the same security as in the humble one we are so very eager to abandon. Examine . . . the conduct of all the greatly misfortunate, and you will find that the misfortunes of by far the greater part of them have arisen from their not knowing when they were well. . . . The inscription on the tombstone of the man who endeavored to mend a tolerable constitution by taking physic: "I was well. I wished to be better; here I am;" may be applied with great justness to the distress of disappointed avarice and ambition. (*TMS*, 150)

The natural counterpoint to our exaggerated estimation of the great is, Smith argued, our natural propensity to shrink back in horror from the poor. By Smith's account, this propensity is so powerful that it inspires "those who have been educated in the higher ranks of life, [to] regard it as worse than death, to be reduced to live, even without labour, upon the same simple fare" as the "meanest labourer" (*TMS*, 50). Likewise, from a natural abhorrence to poverty, a "gentleman" at a "gay assembly" would, Smith observed, "be more mortified to appear covered with filth and rags than with blood and wounds" (*TMS*, 56). Smith attributed our profound revulsion toward "people of poor and mean condition" to our natural inclination to associate poverty with obscurity and isolation. Encounter-

74

ing "human wretchedness," we naturally ignore the possibility that someone might sleep very well in the dingiest hovel and dwell instead on the way that the object of our detestation comes and goes in the world without recognition, never excites sympathy or compassion, and enjoys nobody's respect, affection, or admiration. The real source of our tendency to despise the poor and worship the rich is, consequently, not the material facts of either situation, but our natural desire to be noticed, appreciated, and esteemed.

> From whence, then, arises that emulation which runs through all the different ranks of men, and what are the advantages we propose from that great purpose of human life which we call bettering our condition? To be observed, to be attended to, to be taken notice of with sympathy, complacency, and approbation, are all the advantages we can propose to derive from it. It is the vanity, not the ease, or the pleasure, which interests us. (*TMS*, 50)

What makes our constant effort to better our condition such a potent source of corruption is, Smith asserted, that it frequently inspires us not merely to overvalue the objects of avarice and ambition, but to disguise our truly laudable virtues in an attempt to ape even the lowest characteristics of those who command society's attention. Smith accordingly argued that our natural inclination to imitate our social superiors frequently prompts us to pretend to be more corrupt and dishonest than we actually are. Having raised the "rich and the great" to unmerited heights, we allow them "to set, or to lead, what is called the fashion. Their dress is the fashionable dress; the language of their conversation, the fashionable style; their air and deportment, the fashionable behavior." Given these conditions, "Even their vices and follies are fashionable; and the greater part of men are proud to imitate and resemble them in the very qualities which dishonour and degrade them." Thus, otherwise upright individuals, under the spell of fashion, are apt to mask their better qualities when social elites affect a vulgar style.

> Vain men often give themselves airs of fashionable profligacy, which, in their hearts, they do not approve of, and of which, perhaps, they really are not guilty. They desire to be praised for what they themselves do not think praiseworthy, and are ashamed of unfashionable virtues, which they sometimes practice in secret, and for

which they secretly have some degree of real veneration. There are hypocrites of wealth and greatness, as well as of religion and virtue; and a vain man is apt to pretend to be what he is not, in the one way, as a cunning man is in the other. (*TMS*, 64)

Smith identified two ways to escape the false allure of "place, that great object which divides the wives of aldermen": either one must be morally superior to social opinion or so degraded as to disregard the most primitive standards of social existence. In Smith's view, sensible people might be indifferent to trivial social preferments.

> But rank, distinction, pre-eminence, no man despises, unless he is either raised very much above or sunk very much below, the ordinary standard of human nature; unless he is so confirmed in wisdom and real philosophy, as to be satisfied that, while the propriety of his conduct renders him the just object of approbation, it is of little consequence though he neither be attended to or approved of; or so habituated to the idea of his own meanness, so sunk in slothful and sottish indifference, as entirely to have forgot the desire, and almost the very wish, for superiority. (*TMS*, 185)

While just about all of the members of Smith's society are prone to entertain farfetched ideas about wealth and position, most manage to maintain some portion, and even a significant portion of virtue because they are, for the most part, shut out of the highest ranks and, thereby, insulated from the more virulent temptations attached to social prestige and political power. Unlike those who are born to the loftiest stations, "men in the middling and inferior stations of life" cannot afford to ignore either the rule of law or their standing in their communities; consequently, Smith concluded rather prosaically, "The good old proverb, therefore, That Honesty is the Best Policy, holds in such situations, therefore, we may generally expect a considerable degree of virtue; and fortunately for the good morals of society, these are the situations of by far the greater part of mankind" (*TMS*, 63).[5]

THE "REAL HAPPINESS OF HUMAN LIFE"

Though the great majority of those who come from the middle and lower segments of society remain confined to small communities, a few succeed, through superior knowledge, talent, and "severe and unrelenting application," to rise to political office, where, by dint of the discipline that carried them there, they oblige those who are born to such places to heed their counsel. Smith recounted this scenario in order to explain why those who enter the world without significant social distinctions have always played decisive roles in every government.

> In all governments, accordingly, even in monarchies, the highest
> offices are generally possessed, and the whole detail of administration conducted by men who were educated in middle and inferior
> ranks of life, who have been carried forward by their own industry
> and abilities, though loaded with the jealousy and opposed by the
> resentment, of those who were born their superiors, and to whom
> the great, after having regarded them first with contempt, and afterwards with envy, are at last contented to truckle with the same
> abject meanness with which they desire the rest of mankind should
> behave to themselves. (*TMS*, 63)

On the off chance that these observations might be mistaken for an argument that aristocratic government should be replaced by the rule of "self-made men," it should be emphasized that Smith never supported any departure from the hierarchical practices of "civilized monarchy." Smith may have been "always theoretically a republican," as his biographer John Rae described him, but he grounded his moral theory in his observations of commercial aristocracy and, consistent with his effort to expose the false foundations of social inequality in modern society, ridiculed the petty preoccupations of those who circulate around the vertex of political power.[6] While the "greater part of mankind" manage to maintain a significant degree of virtue, Smith argued, "in the superior stations of life, the case is unhappily not always the same."

> In the courts of princes, in the drawing rooms of the great, where
> success and perferment depend, not upon the esteem of intelligent
> and well-informed equals, but upon the fanciful and foolish favour
> of ignorant, presumptuous, and proud superiors; flattery and falsehood too often prevail over merit and abilities. In such societies, the
> abilities to please, are more regarded than the abilities to serve. . . .
> The external graces, the frivolous accomplishments of that impertinent thing called a man of fashion, are commonly more admired

than the solid and masculine virtues of a warrior, a statesman, a philosopher, or a legislator. (*TMS*, 63)

Smith's disparaging commentary on the silly frivolity and base behavior of the inhabitants of high society might be dismissed as provincial advice to the young men who attended his lectures. However, the trouble with that reading is not only that it underestimates Smith's ambition, but also that it obscures the plain connection between his reflections on the contemptible behavior typical among the most important members of the propertied minority and his general lack of faith in political authority. Smith clearly admired the "masculine" qualities of honorable statesmen and even described the disposition of an effective "reformer and legislator" as the "greatest and noblest of all characters" (*TMS*, 232). Nevertheless, in line with his conviction that corruption prevails in the "superior stations of life," he insisted that the best way for individuals to avoid dependence and disappointment is not to attempt to dedicate themselves to any noble political purpose, but to avoid politics as a vocation. As might be expected from a writer on the outskirts of British society, Smith called on his readers to examine the fate of those who venture down the corridors of political power.

> Of all the discarded statesmen who for their own ease have studied to get the better of ambition, and to despise those honours which they could no longer arrive at, how few have been able to succeed? The greater part have spent their time in the most listless and insipid indolence, chagrined at the thoughts of their own insignificancy . . . without enjoyment, except when they talked of their former greatness, and without satisfaction, except when they are employed in some vain project to recover it. Are you in earnest resolved never to barter your liberty for the lordly servitude of a court, but to live free, fearless, and independent? There seems to be but one way to continue in that virtuous resolution. . . . Never enter the place from whence so few have been able to return; never come within the circle of ambition; nor ever bring yourself into comparison with those masters of the earth who have already engrossed the attention of half of mankind before you. (*TMS*, 57)

This passage not only reads like a description of Bolingbroke's career, it echoes exactly the regrets that he expressed in the "Spirit of Patriotism."

Surveying the condition of the ruling class in England, Bolingbroke declared that those who had been born to lead no longer deserved that honor because their pride had been supplanted by vanity, and their formerly noble ambitions had been extinguished by avarice and sloth. But whereas Bolingbroke described the degradation of the elite as an historical emergency, Smith accepted vanity, appetite, and illusion as the natural foundations of the "distinctions of ranks, and the order of society" (*TMS*, 61). In a word, what Bolingbroke had defined as a perversion of the natural scheme, Smith designated as a natural and necessary principle of social preservation and prosperity. Thus, in the *Theory of Moral Sentiments*, the apparently vicious tendencies of commercial aristocracy were not vindicated, but they were naturalized. In Smith's world, those who dominate society are, generally speaking, morally corrupt and unworthy of imitation, but they inspire respect and emulation because almost everyone imagines that they must be the happiest, most satisfied, and most deserving members of the social order. It is, according to Smith, this natural but mistaken conviction which prevents almost everyone from seeing that contentment and tranquillity are actually attainable in the lowest stations of life.

> In what constitutes the real happiness of human life [the poor] are in no respect inferior to those who would seem so very much above them. In ease of the body and peace of the mind, all the different ranks are nearly upon a level; and the beggar who suns himself by the side of the highway possesses all that security which kings are fighting for. (*TMS*, 185)

There is, of course, a lapse of logic in this passage to the extent that, in Smith's scheme of things, the beggar would either have to be "confirmed in wisdom and real philosophy" or "sunk into the most slothful and sottish indifference" in order to enjoy his inner peace (*TMS*, 57). Nonetheless, these observations are significant because, as much as they call to mind Mandeville's comparison between the "most unciviliz'd peasant" and the "greatest of kings," Smith's transposition of social roles was conceived, not as slapstick, but as an illustration of the irrational ideas which sustain social hierarchy (*Fable*, 315–16). When Mandeville mixed up high and low, the noble and the vulgar, prime ministers and petty thieves, the humor intended sprang from the certainty that social roles must be attached to essential moral qualities. Likewise, both Bolingbroke and

Hume complained that Walpole's system would turn society upside down by removing the real distinctions between "those in the coaches" and "those upon the boxes,"[7] "gentlemen" and "grubs."[8] But in Smith's work, social stratification is linked, not to any genuine moral differences, but to a nearly universal inability to comprehend the basic facts of lived reality. Since most people fail to understand "what constitutes the real happiness of human life," most are relegated to what Bolingbroke described as "imaginary poverty;" and, while elites suffer most from delusions of destitution, virtually everyone below them mistakenly places satisfaction somewhere higher on the social chain.[9] Smith may have invested these common misconceptions with a moral purpose by identifying social display as the natural object of "that great purpose in life we call bettering our condition," but, in contrast to both Bolingbroke and Hume, he insisted that the distinctions drawn between the few and the many proceed from our natural inability to admit that "all of the different ranks" are, in the final analysis, essentially the same (*TMS*, 99, 50).[10]

In other words, unlike Bolingbroke and Hume, who continued to view moral inequality as an irreducible aspect of the human condition, Smith defined conventional "ideas of nobility, gentry, and family" as symptoms of conceit, distortions of the true uniformity of human nature.[11] Smith might have agreed with Hume that the "skin, pores, muscles, nerves . . . sentiments, actions, and manners" of a "day labourer" differ from those of "a man of quality,"[12] but whereas Hume stressed the depth of such distinctions, Smith emphasized that the ostensible dissimilarities between various social types, between, for example, "a philosopher and a common street porter," are ultimately superficial, the result of accident, education, and vanity, rather than expressions of any natural inequality.[13] Consequently, even though Smith acknowledged that social disparities serve to cement the order of society, he never tired of detailing the false foundations of social superiority.

Along these lines, he repeatedly observed that, because most of remain unaware of our real proximity to happiness, most of us spend almost all of our lives laboring under the illusion that wealth and position must lead, sooner or later, to real satisfaction. However, he argued, in times of illness or melancholy, or in the fatigue of old age, our anxious illusions crumble; in these lucid moments, to paraphrase one of Smith's most avid readers, "all that is solid melts into air," and individuals are compelled to confront the real equality of human experience.

In the languor of disease and the weariness of old age, . . . power and riches . . . appear then to be what they really are, enormous and operose machines, contrived to produce a few trifling conveniences to the body . . . which, in spite of all our care, are ready at every moment to burst into pieces, and to crush in their ruins, their unfortunate possessor. They are immense fabrics, which it requires the labour of a life to raise; and which threaten at every moment to overwhelm the person that dwells in them . . . and which, while they stand, leave him always as much, if not more exposed than before, to anxiety, to fear, and to sorrow; to diseases, to danger, and to death. (*TMS*, 182)

That most members of society ordinarily remain oblivious to the true distinctions between contentment and anxiety, safety and insecurity, hardly seems fair. There is, however, nothing in Smith's doctrine which requires nature itself to conform to what human beings naturally tend to regard as right and proper. On the contrary, Smith argued, the "industrious knave cultivates the soil; the indolent good man leaves it uncultivated. Who ought to reap the harvest? who starve and who live in plenty? The natural course of things decides in favour of the knave: the natural sentiments of mankind in favour of the man of virtue" As much as we may try to alter the cruelties of nature, as hard as we may endeavor to avert the "arrow that is aimed at the head of the righteous," nature must prevail, no matter how far it may grieve and enrage our natural sense of justice and sympathy. To suppose otherwise would be to imagine that the preservation and prosperity of humanity should depend on the weak assumptions of reason or the rare injunctions of refined emotion (*TMS*, 168). Our natural tendency to venerate wealth and despise poverty certainly violates even the least reflective code of common morality; nonetheless, Smith observed, however much we might trumpet the virtues of compassion and charity, we must recognize that the "peace and order of society, is of more importance than the relief of the miserable." Therefore, despite the moralists who rightly warn us against the "fascination of greatness," we can only surmise that

> nature has wisely judged that the distinction of ranks, the peace and order of society, would rest more securely upon the plain and palpable difference of wealth and fortune, than upon the invisible and

often uncertain difference of wisdom and virtue. The undistinguish-
ing eyes of the great mob of mankind can well enough perceive the
former; it is with difficulty that the nice discernment of the wise
and the virtuous can sometimes distinguish the latter. In the order
of all those recommendations, the benevolent wisdom of nature is
equally evident. (*TMS*, 226)

Likewise, in view of the "coarse clay of which the bulk of mankind are
formed," it is obvious, Smith argued, that however much it may sometimes injure our feelings or betray our sense of common decency, we must
submit to the superior wisdom of nature's providential plan.

The natural course of things cannot be entirely controlled by the
impotent endeavors of man: the current is too strong and too rapid
for him to stop it; and though the rules which direct it appear to
have been established for the wisest and best purposes, they sometimes produce effects which shock all of his natural sentiments . . .
that every end should be acquired by those means only that Nature
has established, seems to be a rule not only necessary and unavoidable in itself, but useful and proper for rousing the attention and
industry of mankind. (*TMS*, 168–69)

FROM MORAL PHILOSOPHY TO POLITICAL ECONOMY

The preceding arguments indicate, on one hand, Smith's profound perception of the injury, ignorance, and injustice involved in the natural
course of things and, on the other, his steady conviction that these misfor-
tunes are not only inevitable, but utterly indispensable to the general well-
being of humanity at large. Though Smith's calendar of evils may seem
uncommonly crowded, it follows from his endless preoccupation with the
"weakness and folly of man." Smith's aim, in other words, was not by
any stretch to minimize the scope of human imperfection, but to explain
how our natural misconceptions help to advance the true purpose of our
existence, which is to contribute, knowingly or not, to the progress of our
species.

Smith's commentary on the fantasies which "rouse the attention and
industry of mankind" can be compared to his remarks on the social utility
of our natural fear of death. Though there is, he noted, no reason to

suppose that the dead actually experience the decomposition of their flesh and bones, we naturally tend to imagine what it would be like if "our own living souls" were trapped in "their inanimate bodies." As illogical as this nightmare may be, "It is from this very illusion of the imagination, that the foresight of our own dissolution . . . makes us miserable while we are alive." Our anguish about the prospect of our own demise, however much it might proceed from the implausible idea that we might remain conscious as we molder in our graves, is, nonetheless, a profound and necessary source of self-control, since, by threatening us with horrible visions of bodily decay, it naturally teaches us to be wary of violent or socially destructive behavior. In this vein, Smith concluded: "From thence arises one of the most important principles in human nature, the dread of death, the great poison to the happiness, but the great restraint upon the injustice of mankind, which, while it afflicts and mortifies the individual, guards and protects the society" (*TMS*, 13).[14]

In keeping with his effort to illustrate the social utility of illusion, Smith's preoccupation with the anxiety, unhappiness, and corruption that the deceptive desire for affluence visits upon individuals did not prevent him from insisting that these private drawbacks are entirely overshadowed by public benefits.[15] In a much-quoted passage, Smith described the grand advantages derived from the natural but mistaken belief that the chase after wealth and power might relieve our insatiable desires.

> It is well that nature imposes on us in this manner. It is this deception which rouses and keeps in continual motion the industry of mankind. It is this which first prompted them to cultivate the ground, to build houses, to found cities and commonwealths, and to invent and improve all the arts and sciences which ennoble human life . . . the earth by these labours of mankind has been obliged . . . to maintain a greater number of inhabitants . . . the produce of the soil maintains at all times nearly that number of inhabitants which it is capable of maintaining. The rich only select from the heap what is most precious and agreeable. . . . Though the sole end which they propose from the labours of all the thousands whom they employ be the gratification of their own vain and insatiable desires, they divide with the poor the produce of all their improvements. They are led by an invisible hand to make nearly the same distribution of all the necessaries of life . . . had the earth been divided into equal proportions among all its inhabitants, and thus,

THE RULE OF THE RICH?

without knowing it, without intending it, advance the interests of society, and afford the means for the multiplication of the species. (*TMS*, 183–84)

In this crucial passage, Smith directly anticipated the deterministic interpretation of history elaborated throughout the *Wealth of Nations*. He introduced, along with the metaphor of the "invisible hand," his general conception of social evolution as an essentially uncontrolled process, motivated by the pecuniary pursuits of unwitting individuals, and characterized by a constant increase in overall prosperity. Just as he here attributed social, economic, and political development to actions taken to gratify the "vain and insatiable desires" of purely self-regarding individuals, he argued throughout the *Wealth of Nations* that the "natural progress of opulence" automatically proceeds from efforts expended in response to the "vulgar" and "obvious" "desire of bettering our own condition," a passion which "comes with us from the womb, and never leaves us till we go to the grave."[16] As every member of society endlessly endeavors to satisfy this desire,

he necessarily labours to render the annual revenue of the society as great as he can. He generally, indeed, neither intends to promote the public interest, nor knows how much he is promoting it . . . he intends only his own gain, and he is in this, as in many other cases, led by an invisible hand to promote an end which was no part of his intention. Nor is it always the worse for society that it was no part of it. By pursuing his own interest, he frequently promotes that of the society more effectually than when he really intends to promote it.[17]

The concept of unintended benefits set forth here exemplifies the steady agreement between Smith's moral philosophy and his political economy. In the *Theory of Moral Sentiments*, Smith's central goal was to work out the moral consequences of the primacy of the passion for private gain; in the *Wealth of Nations*, his purpose was to elucidate the political and economic implications of that moral limitation.[18] In line with his observations on the social utility of imperfection in his moral theory, the basic proposition of his economic theory was that our constant efforts to better our own condition naturally counteract our inability to foresee, comprehend, or determine the consequences of our actions. Thus, he insisted that self-interest—the very defect which prevents us from perceiving the public good—automatically obliges us to contribute our utmost to the general welfare of society.

> The natural effort of every individual to better his own condition, when suffered to exert itself with freedom and security, is so powerful a principle that it is alone, and without any assistance, not only capable of carrying the society to wealth and prosperity, but of surmounting a hundred impertinent obstructions with which the folly of human laws all too often encumbers its operations.[19]

What is, of course, missing from this picture is any suggestion that social evolution might require significant cooperation, let alone direction, from any human agency. Within the context of eighteenth-century aristocratic society, Smith's insight into the instinctive pursuit of private gain was not that it showed that every member of society is equally capable of rational conduct and, therefore, deserved to be included in the political sphere, but that political elites, the people who throw "impertinent obstructions" into the natural path of progress, are, broadly speaking, extraneous to the natural scheme of things, however much they might try to alter the laws of human behavior or pretend to control the wealth of nations. Thus, against Bolingbroke's conviction that economic self-interest would destroy the aristocracy and, thereby, corrupt the rest of society, and in contrast to Hume's conviction that the avidity for personal possessions must be disciplined by established authority, Smith asserted that limitless desire obviates not only the need for political discipline, but the very idea that ministers, kings, and assorted elites might be responsible for social preservation and prosperity.

> It is the highest impertinence and presumption, therefore, in kings and ministers, to pretend to watch over the economy of private people. . . . They are themselves always, and without any exception, the greatest spendthrifts in the society. Let them look after their own expense, and they may safely trust private people with theirs. If their own extravagance does not ruin the state, that of their subjects never will.[20]

OPULENCE AND OBLIVION

In line with his low opinion of social and political leaders, Smith's account of the transition from feudal to commercial society was designed to illustrate the incapacities of those who place themselves at the head of social order. Against the conventional belief that social development must depend in some way on the caliber or foresight of political or social elites, Smith made every effort to show that the historical evolution of commercial institutions advanced, not as a result of any political policy or plan, but because everyone who pretended to exert authority and control society had not the slightest notion of what was actually coming to pass. According to Smith, the development of trade between town and country was the key to the dissolution of the feudal system. With the expansion of trade, the great proprietors of the period were given the opportunity to exchange their stagnant holdings for money which could, in turn, be exchanged for luxury goods. Thus they were lured into releasing their dependents in order to expend the returns from their lands on items intended for purely personal consumption.

> All for ourselves and nothing for other people, seems, in every age of the world, to have been the vile maxim of the masters of mankind. As soon, therefore as [the great proprietors] could find a method of consuming the whole value of their rents themselves, they had no disposition to share them. . . . For a pair of diamond buckles, perhaps, they exchanged . . . the price of the maintenance of a thousand men for a year, and with it, the whole weight and authority which it could give them . . . for the gratification of the most childish, the meanest, and the most sordid of all vanities, they gradually bartered away their whole power and authority.[21]

As they frittered away the foundation of their military and political power, the great proprietors were gradually reduced to the level of ordinary citizens and, as such, could do nothing to prevent the establishment of "order and good government, and with them, the liberty and security of individuals."[22] The moral of Smith's story was, as usual, that the myopic pursuit of personal interest automatically administers to the prosperity and well-being of the general public.

> A revolution of the greatest importance to the public happiness was, in this manner, brought about by two different orders of people

who had not the least intention of serving the public. To gratify the most childish vanity was the sole motive of the great proprietors. The merchants and manufacturers, much less ridiculous, acted merely from a view of their own interest, and in pursuit of their pedlar principle of turning a penny wherever a penny was to be got. Neither of them had any knowledge or foresight of that great revolution which the folly of the one, and the industry of the other, was gradually bringing about.[23]

Smith's description of the political revolution wrought by the decline of feudalism has been interpreted as an attempt to draw a necessary connection between the rise of commerce and the progress of political liberty.[24] In fact, the political prognosis presented in the *Wealth of Nations* makes it plain that Smith harbored no such hope. Having concluded that the ends of our existence are essentially economic, and having further concluded that we achieve these ends through the automatic operation of our passions, he had no inclination to search for antidotes to the vile practices of the "masters of mankind." Smith's attitude toward political oppression was accordingly resigned.

> The violence and injustice of the rulers of mankind is a ancient evil for which, I am afraid, the nature of human affairs can scarce admit of a remedy. But the mean rapacity, the monopolizing spirit of merchants and manufactures, who neither are, nor ought to be the rulers of mankind, though it cannot perhaps be corrected, may easily be prevented from disturbing the tranquillity of anybody but themselves.[25]

The method Smith proposed to disarm the "monopolizing spirit of merchants and manufacturers" was, of course, to free the economy from "all systems of preference or restraint."[26] The goal he had in mind was not to ensure individual freedom, but to strengthen "order and good government," in other words, stability of possession. The contrast between negative and positive liberty might present itself at this juncture; the trouble with that approach is that it tends to obscure the fact that Smith's arguments were designed to convey the political price of moral infirmity. If Smith emphasized that this infirmity displayed a rational aspect from a social point of view, if he implied an ultimate coincidence between "interest" and "passion," he was still defining a profound moral and political problem.[27] When he stressed the social benefits of appetite and illusion and observed that self-interested individuals accomplish social objectives far beyond their own limited comprehension, he never meant to suggest that moral oblivion might somehow translate into freedom. Instead, he was trying to explain how society survives and prospers despite the disabilities induced by the distortions of insatiable desire.

In his analysis of the "three great, original and constituent orders of every civilized society," that is, landlords, laborers, and merchants and manufacturers, Smith made it abundantly clear that the structure of commercial society serves not as a solution to the moral and political weaknesses embedded in the pursuit of private gain but as an active invitation to moral and political corruption. More specifically, he insisted that the commercial activities peculiar to each of these orders damage each so severely as to render each incapable of dealing in a just or proper manner with any significant political question. Of landlords, Smith wrote:

> When the public deliberates concerning any regulation of commerce or police, the proprietors of land can never mislead it, with a view to promoting the interest of their own particular order; at least if they have any tolerable knowledge of that interest. They are, indeed, too often defective in this tolerable knowledge. They are the only one of the three orders whose revenue costs them neither labour nor care, but comes to them, as it were, of its own accord, and independent of any plan or project of their own. That indolence, which is the natural effect of the ease and security of their situation, renders them too often, not only ignorant, but incapable of that application of mind which is necessary in order to foresee and understand the consequences of any public regulation.[28]

Having excluded those who live by rent from effective participation in the political sphere, Smith proceeded to exclude the majority of society, those who live by wages.

> But though the interest of the labourer is strictly connected with that of the society, he is incapable of comprehending that interest, or of understanding its connection with his own. His condition leaves him no time to receive the necessary information, and his education and his habits are such as to render him unfit to judge

even though he was fully informed. In public deliberations, therefore, his voice is little heard and less regarded.[29]

These conclusions are reinforced in Smith's caustic comments on the demoralizing effects of highly specialized production. On one hand, Smith argued, the development of the division of labor in "every civilized society" furnishes the average worker with luxuries to rival those of an "African king"; on the other hand, this development naturally debilitates that worker as he devotes his life to producing such things as a tenth of a pin.

> The man whose whole life is spent performing a few simple operations has no occasion to exert his understanding. . . . He naturally loses, therefore, the habit of such exertion, and generally becomes as stupid and ignorant as it is possible for a human creature to become . . . Of the great and extensive interests of his country, he is altogether incapable of judging.[30]

In contrast to those who live by rent and wages, those who live by profits are, according to Smith, acutely aware of their own particular political interests. But, unfortunately, insofar as the thoughts of the individuals who make up this order are

> commonly exercised about the interest of their own branch of business, rather than about that of the society . . . the proposal of any new law or regulation of commerce which comes from this order, ought always to be listened to . . . with the most suspicious attention. It comes from an order of men whose interest is never exactly the same with that of the public, who generally have an interest to deceive and even to oppress the public, and who accordingly have, upon many occasions, both deceived and oppressed it.[31]

It is hard to imagine how Smith could have stated his conclusions in more politically problematic and socially comprehensive terms. These are, after all, the "three great, original and constituent orders of every civilized society"; and Smith's unequivocal position on all of these orders is that each is so politically untrustworthy that none can be relied on to rise above and regulate the pursuit of private gain. Smith's case for the "system of natural liberty" was thus not an anticipation of a more egalitarian society or an effort to extend political capacity throughout the social order. Instead, his analysis of what is and what is not essential to the natural progress of opulence was designed to illustrate exactly what he said it was designed to illustrate, namely, that "natural liberty," the latitude to follow the dictates of nature, rather than bend our behavior to the misguided prescriptions of incompetent ministers and politicians, is the most effective way to secure the preservation and prosperity of society.

This is, it should be emphasized, an argument about imperfection rather than moral improvement. Smith's very keen appreciation of the comforts, luxuries, and conveniences produced by the pursuit of personal advantage never led him to doubt that it would be better if more people had the wherewithal to reach for more meaningful goals. His economic theory was not, however, offered as a cure for the corrupting effects of commercial interaction, but as an explanation of the way our natural limitations allow us, without intending any other end except our own "childish," "sordid," "vulgar," "obvious," "frivolous," "mean," or "contemptible," gratification, to contribute as much as is humanly possible to social development. Throughout the *Wealth of Nations*, he defended the natural effort of every individual to better his condition, not as an end in itself, not as a source of individual fulfillment, but as the only available way to overcome the impotence of political practice and power. Consequently, however much Smith may have preferred agrarian to commercial society, the country to the city, land to more modern forms of wealth, his point was that our moral preferences are simply not pertinent to nature's superior plan. When Smith pointed out, time and again, that individuals accomplish social aims without knowing, willing, or intending that purpose, Smith was not suggesting that lack of awareness is good for human beings; he was trying to demonstrate that the natural inability of individuals in general and elites in particular to achieve political virtue promoted rather than prevented economic growth. The novelty of this argument, particularly within the context of aristocratic society, was his claim that those who seem to possess the highest authority, are, in fact, even more oblivious to the public interest than everyone else.

> The statesman, who should attempt to direct private people in what manner they ought to employ their capitals, would not only load himself with a most unnecessary attention, but assume an authority which could safely be trusted, not only to no single person, but to no council or senate whatever, and which would nowhere be more

dangerous than in the hands of a man who had folly and presumption enough to fancy himself fit to exercise it.[32]

POLITICAL INCOMPETENCE AND FREE ENTERPRISE

Since Smith was, in a way, delegitimizing the social and political establishment of the nation, he never expected his theoretical suggestions to meet with much practical success. He accordingly remarked that, as much as he might wish that the aristocratic leaders of Great Britain would quit interfering in the natural course of things, it would be just as "absurd to expect that an Oceana or Utopia" would be set up in their country. Echoing the civic humanist critics of Court Whig oligarchy, he asserted that freedom of trade would forever remain a remote possibility, not only because it would violate the "prejudices of the publick," but because, "what is much more unconquerable, the private interests of many individuals . . . irresistibly oppose it." The master manufacturers Smith put at the head of this opposition had, in his view, amassed so much social and political influence that, "like an overgrown standing army, they have become formidable to the government, and upon many occasions intimidate the legislature." In the face of such imperious power, it would be preposterous to rely on the members of parliament to sacrifice their personal interests to promote the interests of the public. They had, Smith concluded, too much to gain by placing themselves in the service of the monopolists and too much to lose by attempting to take a higher road.

> The member of parliament who supports every proposal for strengthening this monopoly, is sure to acquire not only the reputation of understanding trade, but great popularity and influence with an order of men whose numbers and wealth render them of great importance. If he opposes them, on the contrary, and still more if he has authority enough to be able to thwart them, neither the most acknowledged probity, nor the highest rank, nor the greatest public services can protect him from the most infamous abuse and detraction, from personal insults, nor sometimes from real danger, arising from the insolent outrage of furious and disappointed monopolists.[33]

While Smith regarded the patriotic public service Bolingbroke had called for as a patent impossibility, he was, of course, quick to point out that, despite its political ill effects, the natural and universal pursuit of private interest counteracts the problems which must pervade every political system. Whatever misguided policies politicians might pursue, either to pump up their popularity or to illustrate their integrity, nature steps in to rescue society from even the most burdensome aspects of incompetent government.

> The human body frequently preserves . . . the most perfect state of health under a vast variety of different regimens; even under some which are generally believed to be far from perfectly wholesome . . . in the political body, the natural effort that every individual is continually making to better his own condition is a principle of preservation which is capable of preventing and correcting, in many respects, the bad effect of a political economy both partial and oppressive. Such a political economy, though it no doubt retards, is not always capable of stopping altogether the natural progress of a nation towards wealth and prosperity. If a nation could not prosper without the enjoyment of perfect justice and perfect liberty, there is not a nation in the world which could ever have prospered. In the political body, the wisdom of nature has made ample provision for remedying many of the bad effects of the folly and injustice of man.[34]

Here, as usual, Smith described the pursuit of private interest as a "principle" of social "preservation," not as an individual right. This calls into question another assumption generally made about his case for freedom of trade, namely, that in contrast to mercantilists, Smith conceived of wealth as a private rather than public good.[35] In fact, Smith consistently and explicitly described the pursuit of private interest as evidence of the weakness of human reason, a fountain of individual dissatisfaction, and the most potent source of political ineptitude and corruption. At the same time, throughout his inquiry into the nature and causes of the wealth of nations, he celebrated economic self-interest as the source of historical progress, social improvement, national wealth, and universal plenty. Indeed, Smith was so disengaged from Lockean notions of the pursuit of property that he reduced property ownership in commercial society to a private mirage. Thus, as individuals, the owners of property dream of consuming a whole harvest, but as participants in a social system which is beyond their comprehension, they end up distributing all that is grown in their fields. The spirit and logic of this vision could not be more plain: in line with his general appreciation for the social utility of false ideas, Smith was trying to show that what "afflicts and mortifies the individual, guards and protects the society" (*TMS*, 13). Smith may have emphasized that the affliction and mortification attached to the desire for personal gain was more damaging to the aristocracy than to those who stood below them in the social hierarchy, but it is certainly as difficult to call something "good" because it injures some individuals less than others as it is to inject language about "individual rights" into a discourse on unmet desire.[36]

Of course, if Smith had ever gotten around to reading Marx, he would have realized that the profligate aristocracy was well on its way to the dustbin of history, and that the distinction of ranks in British society was about to be overturned by the principle of abstract equality. Since he was, however, either unwilling or unable to adopt the theoretical standpoint of the nineteenth century, he assumed that the "plain and palpable difference of birth and fortune" would continue to "set one man above another" in commercial society (*TMS*, 226). At the same time, in accordance with his preoccupation with the illusory aspects of social stratification, he surmised not that these admittedly empty distinctions would be replaced by another set of standards, but that modern modes of getting and spending exacerbate the morally debilitating consequences of social and political prominence. In other words, Smith, accepted the permanence of aristocratic ascendancy, but, much like Mandeville, admitted that, "in every civilized society," that is, "in every society in which the distinction of ranks has once been completely established," the habits of the rich and the great render them, in many respects, morally inferior to the majority.

"People of fashion" tend, he argued, to subscribe to a "liberal or, if you will, loose system" of morality, while the system favored by common people is comparatively "strict or austere." Smith clearly preferred austerity to prodigality, but never implied that the gap between these two systems might somehow be closed. Instead, he observed, on one hand, the "wanton" and "even disorderly pursuit of pleasure" typical among the higher ranks is "generally treated with a good deal of indulgence." On the other,

> the vices of levity are always ruinous to the common people, and a single week's thoughtlessness and dissipation is often sufficient to undo a poor man for ever, and to drive him to despair upon com-

THE RULE OF THE RICH?

THE RULE OF THE RICH?

mitting the most enormous crimes. The wiser and better sort of
common people, therefore, have always the utmost abhorrence and
detestation of such excesses, which their experience tells them are so
immediately fatal to people of their condition.[37]

Although Smith scholars have cited these comments as part of a definite campaign for moral and political improvement, nothing in Smith's
analysis implies such deliberate intervention.[38] Instead, in line with his
general tendency to view codes of morality as the products of historical
development and social circumstance, Smith first emphasized the austerity of the common people as a requirement drawn from experience rather
than a value transmitted by instruction. He then proceeded to explain
why the intemperate and excessive inclinations of their superiors are, for
the most part, impervious to correction.

> The disorder and extravagance of several years . . . will not always
> ruin a man of fashion, and people of that rank are very apt to con-
> sider the power of indulging in some degree of excess as one of the
> advantages of their fortune, and the liberty of doing so without
> censure or reproach, as one of the privileges which belong to their
> station, therefore, they regard such excesses with but a small degree
> of disapprobation, and censure them either very slightly or not at
> all.[39]

Smith's disdain for the lifestyles of the rich and famous did not lead
him to exaggerate the dangers that the denizens of high society posed to
general prosperity. Instead, excusing neither the repugnant aspects of their
wasteful ways nor the economic drawbacks of their self-indulgence, he
stressed that they constitute only a tiny minority. "It can seldom happen,"
he wrote, "that the circumstances of a great nations can be much affected
either by the prodigality or misconduct of individuals; the profusion or
imprudence of some being always more than compensated by the frugality
and good conduct of others."[40] In contrast with the "loose" or "liberal"
tendencies of the highest ranks, the "greater part of men" follow the
"vulgar and obvious principle" of improving their condition, doing their
best to "save and accumulate some part of what they acquire, either regu-
larly or annually, or upon some extraordinary occasion." Thus, all of the
resources prodigals throw away on "idle guests and menial servants," are
more than offset by the prudence and productivity of those below them

on the social scale. "Though the principle of expense, therefore, prevails," Smith concluded, "in most men upon some occasions, and in some men on almost all occasions, yet the greater part of men, taking the course of their life at an average, the principle of frugality seems not only to predominate, but to predominate very greatly."[41]

The confidence Smith expressed in the frugality of the many to overcome the extravagance of the few wavered when it came to spendthrift governments. "Great nations are," he asserted, "never impoverished by private, though they sometimes are by publick prodigality and misconduct." To make this point, Smith complained of the crowds of unproductive hands employed in overgrown civil, military, and religious establishments, as well as the revenue wasted on any unusually splendid court. When such unproductive institutions grow so far out of control that the number of people engaged in productive activity begins to drop year after year, the prudence and parsimony of the majority may be, he suggested, entirely negated by the excesses of those at the top of the political order. However, having broadcast this warning against runaway government spending, Smith proceeded to note that such "violent and forced encroachment" on the productivity of society is extremely out of the ordinary. Short-sighted and irresponsible ministers and kings may place a strain on the resources available to more productive people, but, in nearly all cases, the "constant effort of every man to better his condition" cancels out political bungling and waste. Smith accordingly ended his diatribe against improvident monarchy and bloated bureaucracy by repeating his favorite theme: The "frugality and good conduct [of individuals] . . . is upon most occasions, it appears, from experience, sufficient to compensate, not only . . . private prodigality and misconduct . . . but the publick extravagance of government."[42]

Smith's observations on the compensatory effects of popular frugality set the stage for his discussion of the "Expence of Supporting the Dignity of the Sovereign." Once again, in keeping with his skeptical view of government and his consistently incredulous approach to social superiority, he emphasized the distinction of ranks not as an expression of genuine inequality, but as a psychological imperative. At the same time, just in case his readers might not have understood his remarks on the childish desires of the great feudal lords as a comment on contemporary aristocracy, he went out of his way to call attention to the silly and trivial ambitions which animate the highest ranks in modern commercial countries. In the first place, he asserted, anyone who calculates the cost of supporting "civilized monarchy" must recognize that the king cannot be expected to embrace a code of conduct more disciplined than the "loose" and "liberal" lifestyle favored by other people of quality. On the contrary, "in an opulent and improved society," Smith insisted,

> where all the different orders of people are growing more expensive in their houses, in their furniture, in their tables, in their dress, and in their equipage; it cannot well be expected that the sovereign should hold out against the fashion. He naturally, therefore, or rather necessarily becomes more expensive in all those different articles too. His dignity even seems to require that he should become so.[43]

Likewise, in an effort to explain why such a considerable portion of the public revenue must be set aside to prop up the monarch's pride and self-esteem, Smith pointed out that the price of royal dignity is, in effect, determined by the extent of the market for luxury goods. Sovereigns in "rude and primitive" societies might be inclined to practice frugality, but the self-image of any thoroughly modern majesty depends on his consumption of the high-priced baubles and trifles that fascinate those who are, if not exactly his social equals, then, from a material standpoint at least, uncomfortably close.

> In a commercial country abounding with every sort of expensive luxury, the sovereign, in the same manner as almost all the great proprietors in his dominions, naturally spends a great part of his revenue in purchasing those luxuries. His own and the neighboring countries supply him abundantly with all the costly trinkets which compose the splendid, but insignificant pageantry of a court. For the sake of an inferior pageantry of the same kind, his nobles dismiss their retainers, make their tenants independent, and become gradually as insignificant as the greater part of the wealthy burghers in his dominions. The same frivolous passions, which influence his conduct, influence his. How can it be supposed that he should be the only rich man in his dominions who is insensible to pleasures of this kind?[44]

This purely psychological and practically contemptuous approach to royalty might lead some readers to conclude that Smith must have been a republican or, more vaguely, a proponent of some popular form of government. However, Smith's work is not about the redistribution of political authority, but about the ultimate insignificance of political power. Accordingly, rather than suggesting any alternative to civilized monarchy, Smith followed Hume's example by emphasizing that the members of society expect political elites to display the degree of magnificence that is commonly accepted as customary to their rank. Along these lines, he reasoned somewhat dryly: "As in point of dignity, a monarch is more raised above his subjects than the chief magistrate of any republic is ever supposed to be above his fellow citizens; so a greater expence is required to support that higher dignity. We naturally expect more splendor in the court of a king, than in the mansion house of a dodge or burgo-master."[45] In Smith's view, it seems that the provident majority is, in most cases, eager to shoulder the wasteful and sometimes onerous expenses of royal dignity, enhancing social and political stability not only by furnishing the king with some sense of his own superiority, but by making him seem to deserve their obedience and respect.

Smith's biting commentary on the "frivolous passions," "disorderly pursuits," and "mean rapacity" of the wealthiest and most powerful members of the British aristocracy contradicts both his one-time reputation as an overly optimistic apologist for capitalism and his new-found incarnation as a sympathetic defender of the Court Whig regime. His animadversions on masters, merchants, landlords, monarchs, ministers, and other social leaders seem, however, perfectly consistent when viewed in conjunction with the moral problems posed by the commercialization of aristocratic property and with recent studies of the increasing wealth, cohesion, and power of the eighteenth-century British aristocracy. The massive estates, monumental country houses, splendid parks, palatial homes in town, rooms full of elegant objects, galleries of fine paintings, and other forms of conspicuous consumption that old and new aristocrats amassed as testaments to their dignity stand out, in the eyes of present-day historians, as proof of their unprecedented economic, political, and social supremacy.[46] But if these salutes to social hierarchy, along with election returns and financial records, now serve to indicate that aristocrats were both willing and able to flourish in commercial society, such evidence was cited throughout the eighteenth century as evidence of their incompetence as a ruling class.

Thus, while Mandeville made fun of aristocratic corruption in his all too complete definition of luxury, and Bolingbroke affected exaggerated respect for rusticity, Hume dutifully expressed his preference for the "unbought satisfaction of conservation," "health, and "study" over the "worthless toys and gewgaws" of material success.[47] Smith, on the other hand, responded to the social, economic, and political triumph of commercial aristocracy by elaborating a system of moral philosophy and political economy centered on the moral limitations of the highest ranks.

From this standpoint, it is clear that the contrast Smith drew between popular providence and elite prodigality was designed not to resolve the oxymoronic aspects of commercial aristocracy, but to explain how society prospers despite the ignoble and unworthy inclinations that follow from the inheritance or accumulation of any considerable portion of personal wealth and power. Against this, of course, it might be objected that Smith meant to transfer authority from the aristocracy or, if that would overstate the activist impulse in his writings, to suggest that power ought to be exercised by another, possibly larger social class.[48] However, rather than imposing a more recent agenda onto Smith's consciousness, it makes more sense to recognize the unmistakable message he meant to send when he stressed that human beings advance social progress without "knowing, willing, or intending" the outcomes of their actions (*TMS*, 183–84). He was clearly and explicitly dissenting from the aristocratic notion that men of property ought to deserve to serve as the head of the social corpus, the disinterested overseers of the inferior majority. Within the confines of eighteenth-century aristocratic society, this was, of course, not a plea for a more democratic system; it was a repudiation of politics.

Thus, rather than dismissing Mandeville's paradoxical view of the Whig oligarchy, Bolingbroke's alarm about aristocratic immorality, or Hume's consternation about the decay of nobility, Smith rejected authority itself. He did not, in making this move, abandon the fundamental premise of aristocracy, that is, the notion that those who rule *ought* to be materially and morally superior to the rest of society. Rather, having reduced the recognized elite to moral mediocrity, he reduced politics to comparative insignificance and placed wisdom and virtue, which had been seen as essential prerequisites for effective political leadership, at the fringes of social order. He did not, in other words, give up the philosophical rationale for social inequality; instead, seeing no way attach political authority to genuine superiority, he let go of government as the determining factor of social life.

In his exceedingly brief description of the duties of the sovereign, Smith accordingly argued for unrestricted economic competition, not because it would somehow allow the members of society to rise to the level of virtuous or even competent citizens, but because he saw the perpetual effort of individuals to improve their own condition as the only obtainable antidote to the defects of political "knowledge" and "wisdom."

All systems of preference or restraint being thus entirely taken away, the simple and obvious system of natural liberty asserts itself of its own accord. Every man is left perfectly free to pursue his own interest in his own way and to bring his industry or his capital into competition with those of any other man or order of men. The sovereign is completely discharged from a duty, in the attempting to perform which he must always be subject to innumerable delusions, and for the proper performance of which no human wisdom or knowledge could ever be sufficient; the duty of superintending the industry of private people, and of directing it towards the employments most suitable to the interests of society.[49]

This degree of political pessimism can be seen as a logical development from the rather desperate expectations expressed in Bolingbroke's "Idea of a Patriot King." Smith undoubtedly would have agreed with Bolingbroke's assertion that a truly virtuous leader had to be acknowledged as the "most uncommon phenomena in the moral or physical world."[50] But rather than following Mandeville, and translating the scarcity of virtue into gibes against duplicitous politicians, or pinning his hopes, like Hume, on insensible obedience, Smith reacted to commercialization of aristocratic property by accepting the genuine elite, in his words, "a very small party," as socially invisible and politically irrelevant. Confronted with the classical republican critique of commerce as anathema to civic virtue, Smith concluded not that there might be some way to reconcile commercial engagement and political integrity, commercial interdependence and moral autonomy, but that earlier political theorists had exaggerated the reach of reason and had, consequently, understated the role of imperfection in the natural scheme. Thus, in the *Wealth of Nations*, Smith distinguished himself from previous political philosophers, not by resolving the problems posed by commercial aristocracy or by making capitalism safe for modernity, but by becoming the first theorist to provide an essentially negative answer to the question, Who should rule?

Postscript

In the preceding chapters, I have tried to show that Adam Smith's doctrine of limited government can be interpreted as a commentary on the moral limitations of the eighteenth-century British aristocracy. While this interpretation does not provide an exhaustive account of Smith's ideas, it clears up a few of the puzzles surrounding his position in the history of political thought. More specifically, if we recognize that the tensions within commercial aristocracy led Smith to doubt the significance of political authority, but never to question the permanence of social hierarchy, we can see why such a wide range of eighteenth-century writers either implicitly echoed or explicitly confirmed the central themes of his work. There is, for example, no hint of anything approaching Tom Paine's commitment to republicanism in the *Wealth of Nations*; nevertheless, the critique it contains of the frivolous ambitions of noblemen, kings, and politicians can be related to Paine's contention that hereditary government places "man . . . perpetually in contradiction with himself" because it obliges him to "accept . . . for a king, or a chief magistrate, or a legislator, a person whom he would not elect for constable."[1] At the same time, giving full weight to Smith's Humean conception of the "plain and palpable distinctions of rank and fortune" as the ordering principle of social interaction allows us to understand his affinity with deeply conservative thinkers such as Edmund Burke (*TMS*, 226).

Of course, the *Wealth of Nations* stands as such a landmark in the development of political and economic theory, it is possible to relate Smith's writings to those of any number of subsequent thinkers. If we look under "M," for example, James Madison, Karl Marx, and J. S. Mill will all appear before our eyes. In respect to the evolution of classical political economy, however, glancing at the relationship between Smith and Thomas Malthus allows us to see most clearly that, in the wake of the *Wealth of Nations*, economic discourse underwent an immediate and illuminating change. Malthus's *Essay on Population* (1798), which was a direct response to Smith as well as political progressives such as William Godwin, concentrated not on the nature and causes of wealth but on the nature and causes of poverty and, in contrast to Smith's reflections on the ignoble inclinations of the rich, focused almost exclusively on the apparently undisciplined habits of the propertyless majority. Against Smith's assertion that the popular principles of industry and frugality would naturally continue to operate even in the midst of prosperity, Malthus identified the "killing frost of misery" as necessary, not only to keep the majority from multiplying beyond the resources available to keep them alive, but to compel them to maintain a level of productivity sufficient to support society as a whole.[2]

Shifting the focus of political economy from the political incompetence of the few to the moral and physical fortitude of the many enabled Malthus to remove the problem of privation entirely from the purview of the ruling elite and place it squarely on the shoulders of the laboring majority. In contrast to Smith's concern about the social burdens imposed by extravagant courts and spendthrift governments, Malthus maintained that the "principle and most permanent cause of poverty has little or no relation to forms of government or to the unequal division of property . . . as the rich do not in reality possess the power of finding employment and maintenance for the poor, the poor can not, in the nature of things, possess the right to demand them."[3]

Along the same lines, Malthus maintained that the seemingly spineless behavior of parliament in relation to the crown was due not to the members' pursuit of their personal interests, as Smith had asserted, but to their entirely understandable fear of what might happen if hungry mobs of "redundant" laborers fell prey to the delusion that government might be responsible for their woes. "Great as has been the influence of corruption," Malthus admitted,

> I cannot yet think so meanly of the country gentlemen of England as to believe that they would thus have given up a part of their birthright of liberty, if they had not been actuated by a real and genuine fear that it was in greater danger from the people than from the crown. They appeared to surrender themselves to government on condition of being protected from the mob; but they never would have made this melancholy and disheartening surrender, if such a mob had not existed either in reality or imagination.[4]

From the premise that the "country gentlemen" had been motivated "more by fear than by treachery," Malthus concluded that, if the lower ranks "were taught to know how small a part of their present distress was attributable to government, [their] discontent and irritation . . . would be much less to be dreaded, "and the "guardians of British liberty" might then be expected to resume their usual posts.[5]

> The country gentlemen and men of property might securely return to a wholesome jealousy of the encroachments of power; and instead of sacrificing the liberties of the subject on the altar of public safety, might, without any just apprehension of the people, not only tread back their late steps, but firmly insist upon those gradual reforms which . . . the storms of circumstance have rendered necessary, to prevent the gradual destruction of the British constitution.[6]

To appreciate how profoundly the social and political obligations attached to aristocracy changed in the course of the eighteenth century, one has only to imagine how Bolingbroke would have responded to Malthus's effort to blame the common people for the way "the country gentlemen and men of property" had abandoned their "birthright of liberty." It is, after all, hard to see how any "country gentleman" might retain some claim to superiority after admitting that he had failed his civic duty because he had come to fear the humble people he had been born to govern and protect.

As weak as Malthus's justification of "country gentlemen" might seem in comparison to Bolingbroke's celebration of "heroick" virtue, Malthusian population theory provided a remarkably coherent defense of commercial aristocracy. Given the apparent tendency of the poor to increase faster than the means necessary to sustain them, Malthus emphasized that even "under a government constructed upon the best and purest principles, and executed by men of the highest talents and integrity, the most squalid poverty and wretchedness might prevail from the principle of population alone." Having thus delivered commercially-oriented "country gentlemen" from the aspersions cast upon them in works such as the *Fable of the Bees*, *The Idea of a Patriot King*, and the *Wealth of Nations*, Malthus insisted that the only truly rational and generous rule of conduct the upper classes could adopt in respect to those below them would be to relinquish all forms of "indiscriminate charity" and recognize that, "whatever encourages and promotes the habits of industry, prudence, foresight, virtue, and cleanliness, among the poor is beneficial to them and to the country, and whatever removes or diminishes the incitements to any of these qualities is detrimental to the state and pernicious to the individual."[7]

As indicated by the coincidence between the qualities Malthus hoped to instill in the propertyless majority and the lists of moral virtues quoted in the introduction to this book, there seems to be an amazing lack of creativity among writers who like to specify which attributes ought to be possessed by people who possess almost nothing at all. But whatever correspondence there may be between the virtues some theorists wished to drill into the poor at the end of the eighteenth-century and the values others want to implant in the underclass in present-day society, understating the distance between these two moments would clearly be a mistake. Malthus's cut-rate approach to aristocratic ascendancy, which stressed, above all, that the "poor have no right of claim to support," may sound suspiciously like the recent machinations of American "free traders" who, unappeased by the collapse of unions, stagnant wages, massive tax reductions, and relentless cutbacks to programs aimed the poorest members of the population, love to talk about "zeroing out entitlements."[8]

There are, however, obvious differences between the way eighteenth-century writers addressed the relationship between wealth and poverty and the way latter-day commentators have responded to increasing inequality. In the first case, the commercial activities of the Whig oligarchy convinced writers such as Smith and Malthus that the propertied few were neither willing nor able to foster the material well-being of the laboring majority. In our own time, the pressures of international capitalism have persuaded many observers to conclude that the growing gap between the rich and the poor lies largely beyond the reach of politics.[9] Admittedly, theorists of both historical moments surmised that markets rather than governments should determine who would occupy the top of the social structure and who would languish down below. In the first case, however, the turn toward market mechanisms unhinged aristocratic property from long-standing notions about nobility, benevolence, protection, and charity. In the second, the elevation of market forces over political institutions has relieved elites from many of the pressures once imposed by popular opposition to free enterprise.[10]

Whatever similarities one may detect between these two situations, the contrast between them clearly lies in over two hundred years of popular resistance to the destructive results of capitalist competition. The major social movements of the past two centuries certainly never achieved the utopia that philosophers and activists once envisioned, but they did promote defenses ranging from minimum wage legislation to workplace safety regulations to legal recourse against various forms of intimidation, harassment and discrimination. Of course, when Smith set forth his "system of natural liberty," he never imagined that the propertyless majority would ever wrest such concessions from the propertied minority. From the vantage point of the late eighteenth-century, when, as Smith put it, the voice of the typical worker was "little heard and less regarded," no one could predict that strikes, boycotts, insurrections, sit-ins, demonstrations, and other forms of popular insubordination would fundamentally alter the distribution of wealth and transform the political sphere.[11] From the vantage point of post-industrial society, when, as evidenced in the bending of governments everywhere to the commands of capitalist consolidation, it seems that ordinary people—the millions who vie for low-wage jobs so that elites can rest easy about inflation and who bear the brunt of "austerity budgets" in the aftermath of tax cuts and bailouts of global corporations—must learn to expect a great deal less from democratic politics. Thus capitalism, which once enriched aristocrats but, ultimately, destroyed aristocracy, currently presents new threats to what passes for democracy. In the unlikely event that the few who are amassing astonishing wealth in this unhappy system are ever obliged to explain themselves to the rest of the population, they could reach back to the *Wealth of Nations*, if not for a real defense, then at least for the excuse that their moral defects kept them from choosing more meaningful lives.

NOTES

Introduction

1. See Edward N. Wolff, *Top Heavy: A Study of the Increasing Inequality of Wealth in America* (New York: The Twentieth Century Fund, 1995); Reynolds Farley, *The New American Reality* (New York: Russell Sage Foundation, 1996); Donald L. Bartlett and James B. Steel, *America: What Went Wrong?* (Kansas City: Andrews and McMeel, 1992); Sheldon Danziger and Peter Gottschalk, eds., *Uneven Tides: Rising Inequality in America* (New York: Russell Sage Foundation, 1993); idem, *America Unequal* (Cambridge, Mass.: Harvard University Press, 1995); Sherri Matteo, ed., *American Women in the Nineties: Today's Critical Issues* (Boston: Northeastern University Press, 1993); Jeffrey Madrick, *The End of Affluence: The Causes and Consequences of America's Economic Decline* (New York Random House, 1995); and Derek Bok, *The State of the Nation: Government and the Quest for a Better Society* (Cambridge, Mass.: Harvard University Press, 1996).

2. See Richard J. Herrnstein and Charles Murray, *The Bell Curve: Intelligence and Class Structure in American Life* (New York: The Free Press, 1994).

3. Charles de Montalembert, "A Gentlemanly Rule—Not A Bureaucratic System," in *The English Ruling Class*, ed. W. L. Guttman (London: Weidenfeld and Nicholson, 1969), 34.

4. See Peter Laslett, *The World We Have Lost: England Before the Industrial Age* (New York: Charles Scribner's Sons, 1965); and idem, *The World We Have Lost: Further Explored* (New York: Charles Scribner's Sons, 1984).

5. See David Cannadine, *Aspects of Aristocracy: Grandeur and Decline in Modern Britain* (New Haven: Yale University Press, 1994); idem, *The Decline and Fall of the British Aristocracy* (New Haven: Yale University Press, 1990); Linda Colley, *Britons: Forging the Nation, 1707–1837* (New Haven: Yale University Press, 1992); Robert Brenner, "Bourgeois Revolution and the Transition to Capitalism," in *The First Modern Society: Essays in English History in Honour of Lawrence Stone*, ed. A. L. Beier, David Cannadine, and James M. Rosenheim (Cambridge: Cambridge University Press, 1989); Daniel A. Baugh, *Aristocratic Government and Society in Eighteenth-Century England: The Foundations of Stability* (New York: New Viewpoints, 1975); Negley Harte and Roland Quinault, eds., *Land and Society in Britain, 1700–1914: Essays in Honour of F. M. L. Thompson* (Manchester and New York: Manchester University Press, 1996); and J. H. Plumb, *The Origins of Political Stability in England, 1675–1725* (Boston: Houghton Mifflin Company, 1967).

6. See E. P. Thompson, *Customs in Common* (London: The Merlin Press, 1991); idem, *Whigs and Hunters: The Origin of the Black Act* (New York: Pantheon Books, 1975); John Brewer and John Styles, eds., *An Ungovernable People: The English and Their Law in the Seventeenth and Eighteenth Centuries* (New Brunswick: Rutgers University Press, 1980); and Lee Davidson, Tim Hitchcock, Tim Keirn, and Robert Shoemaker, eds., *Stilling the Grumbling Hive: The Response to Social and Economic Problems in England, 1689–1870* (New York: St. Martin's Press, 1992).

7. Istvan Hont and Michael Ignatieff, "Needs and Justice in the *Wealth of Nations*: An Introductory Essay," in *Wealth and Virtue: The Shaping of Political Economy in the Scottish Enlightenment*, ed. Istvan Hont and Michael Ignatieff (Cambridge: Cambridge University Press, 1983), 15.

8. Adam Smith, *An Inquiry into the Nature and Causes of the Wealth of Nations*, ed. R. H. Campbell and A. S. Skinner, 2 vols. (Indianapolis: Liberty Classics, 1976), vol. 1, book I, p. 37.

9. See Colley, *Britons: Forging the Nation, 1707–1837*; Peter Earle, *The Making of the English Middle Class: Business, Society, and Family Life in London, 1660–1730* (Berkeley and Los Angeles: University of California Press, 1989); Marjorie Morgan, *Manners, Morals, and Class in England, 1774–1858* (New York: St. Martin's Press, 1994); and W. D. Rubenstein, "Businessmen into Landowners: The Question Revisited," in *Land and Society in Britain*, ed. Harte and Quinault.

10. Edmund Burke, "Thoughts and Details on Scarcity—Originally Presented to the Right Hon. William Pitt, in the Month of November, 1795," *The Works of Edmund Burke, With a Memoir*, 2 vols. (New York: Harper and Brothers, Publishers, 1854), 2:181.

11. Gertrude Himmelfarb, *The De-Moralization of Society: From Victorian Virtues to Modern Values* (New York: Alfred A. Knopf, 1995), 29, 261.

12. See James Tully and Quentin Skinner, eds., *Meaning and Context: Quentin Skinner and His Critics* (Princeton: Princeton University Press, 1988); John Dunn, *Rethinking Modern Political Theory* (Cambridge: Cambridge University Press, 1985); and J. G. A. Pocock, *Virtue, Commerce, and History: Essays on Political Thought and History, Chiefly in the Eighteenth Century* (Cambridge: Cambridge University Press, 1985).

Like these scholars, I think it is possible to understand historical texts as deliberate productions, the intentional creations of people who actually existed. In contrast to Pocock's preoccupation with ideological "persistence," however, my reading of Mandeville, Bolingbroke, Hume, and Smith is colored not so much by the fact that these authors lived in the eighteenth century as by the fact that they died there, too.

Chapter 1

1. In case some postmodernist readers require a translation of this thesis, perhaps I should say that problematizing the concept of moral authority in certain canonical contributions to contemporary discourse on eighteenth-century commercial society elicits the suspicion that classical political economy achieved canonicity only by delegitimizing the intertextual conventions developed to formalize aristocratic rule. For postmodern views of a group of texts, including the *Theory of Moral Sentiments* (ed. D. D. Raphael and A. L. Macfie [Indianapolis: Liberty Press, 1982] [hereafter cited as *TMS*]) and the *Wealth of Nations* (ed. R. H. Campbell and A. S. Skinner, 2 vols. [Indianapolis: Liberty Classics, 1976] [hereafter cited as *WN*]), that somehow appeared in the eighteenth century, see Vivienne Brown, *Adam Smith's Discourse: Canonicity, Commerce, and Conscience* (London: Routledge, 1994). For a truly heroic "confrontation" with the so-called Adam Smith, see Michael J. Shapiro, *Reading "Adam Smith": Desire, History, and Value* (New York: Sage Publications, 1993).

2. The title of Chapter 1 is designed to recall Joseph Cropsey's treatment of Smith's contribution to political philosophy in *Polity and Economy: An Interpretation of the Principles of Adam Smith* (The Hague: Nijhoff, 1957). Although it preceded the republican paradigm, Cropsey's work continues to stand out as one of the most insightful readings of Smith's writings, illustrating that those who approach the free market system without the burden of democratic expectations, such as F. A. Hayek, for example, generally provide the most convincing accounts of the evolution of classical liberal political thought. See F. A. Hayek, *The Road to Serfdom* (New York: Routledge and Kegan Paul, 1944); and idem, *New Studies in Philosophy, Politics, Economics, and the History of Ideas* (Chicago: University of Chicago Press, 1978).

This observation is not by any means meant to echo the increasingly popular notion that the collapse of Marxism, as both an approach to history and a guide to the future of capitalist society, somehow proves that the conclusions of anti-Marxism must have been correct. See, for example, Frank Hahn, "On Some Economic Limits to Politics," in *The Economic Limits to Politics*, ed. John Dunn (Cambridge: Cambridge University Press, 1990), 142–64. Hahn reluctantly adopts Hayek's convictions about the need to subject people to economic coercion in order to make them produce the basic necessities of life. In *Revising State Theory: Essays in Politics and Post-Industrialism* (Philadelphia: Temple University Press, 1987), Fred Block builds on the work of Karl Polanyi in order to point out that such a degree of submission to market forces would destroy the world. For confirmation of Block's conclusions about the effects of unrestrained capitalist competition, see the New Jersey Turnpike, especially Exits 13A to 14C; and Fred Block, "Contradictions of Self-Regulating Markets," in *The Legacy of Karl Polanyi*, ed. Marguerite Mendell and Daniel Salee (New York: St. Martin's Press, 1991).

3. See Lee Davidson, Tim Hitchcock, Tim Keirn, and Robert Shoemaker, eds. *Stilling the Grumbling Hive: The Response to Social and Economic Problems in England, 1689–1870* (New York: St. Martin's Press, 1992); A. L. Beier, "Poverty and Progress in Early Modern England," in *The First Modern Society: Essays in English History in Honour of Lawrence Stone*, ed. A. L. Beier, David Cannadine, and James M. Rosenheim (Cambridge: Cambridge University Press, 1989); and J. C. D. Clark, *Revolution and Rebellion: State and Society in England During the Seventeenth and Eighteenth Centuries* (Cambridge: Cambridge University Press, 1986).

4. See J. G. A. Pocock, *Virtue, Commerce, and History: Essays on Political Thought and History, Chiefly in the Eighteenth Century* (Cambridge: Cambridge University Press, 1985); J. H. Plumb, *The Origins of Political Stability: England, 1675–1725* (Boston: Houghton Mifflin, 1967); John Cannon, ed., *The Whig Ascendancy: Colloquies on Hanoverian England* (London: Edward Arnold, 1981); Henry Horowitz, "Liberty, Law, and Property, 1689–1776," in *Liberty Secured?: Britain Before and After 1688*, ed. J. R. Jones (Stanford: Stanford University Press, 1992; Neil McKendrick, ed., *Historical Perspectives: Studies in English Thought and Society in Honour of J. H. Plumb* (London: Europa Publishers, 1974); Jeremy Black, ed., *Britain in the Age of Walpole* (New York: St. Martin's Press, 1984); idem, *British Politics from Walpole to Pitt, 1741–1789* (New York: St. Martin's Press, 1990); and Daniel A. Baugh, ed., *Aristocratic Government and Society in Eighteenth-Century England: The Foundations of Stability* (New York: New Viewpoints, 1975).

5. See John Barrel, *The Political Theory of Painting from Reynolds to Hazlitt: The "Body of the Public"* (New Haven: Yale University Press, 1986); idem, *The Birth of Pandora and the Division of Knowledge* (Philadelphia: University of Pennsylvania Press, 1992); David H. Solkin, *Painting for Money: The Visual Arts and the Public Sphere in Eighteenth-Century England* (New Haven: Yale University Press, 1993); Jean-Christophe Agnew, *Worlds Apart: The Market and the Theater in Anglo-American Thought, 1550–1750* (Cambridge: Cambridge University Press, 1986); James Raven, "Defending Conduct and Property: The London Press and the Luxury Debate," in *Early Modern Conceptions of Property*, ed. John Brewer and Susan Staves (New York: Routledge, 1995); and Lawrence E. Klein, "Property and Politeness in the Early Eighteenth-Century Whig Moralists: The Case of the Spectator," in *Early Modern Conceptions of Property*, ed. Brewer and Staves.

6. Pocock inveighs against "bourgeois" in his review of Isaac Kramnick, *Republicanism and Bourgeois Radicalism: Political Ideology in Late Eighteenth-Century England and America* (see *Eighteenth-Century Studies* 25, no. 2 [winter 1991–92]). In his final paragraph, Pocock congratulates Kramnick for his progressive politics, but goes on to say, "I could wish he sounded less like the sniveling Stalinists of my youth, who told me that democracy was an ideology for slaveholders; a view I once heard echoed by a black woman novelist (who shall be nameless) in the only full-bloodedly fascist speech I have listened to in America." I do not want to malign

Pocock as racist, sexist, or antinovelist, but it is unclear why he supposes that adding the words "black woman novelist" somehow helps to indicate what was so "full-bloodedly fascist" about this unnamed writer's speech. To test this lack of clarity, try substituting a less descriptive phrase for "black woman novelist"; for example, "a view I once overhead in an airport bar" or "a view I once heard echoed by a passenger on a bus."

7. Examples of Court Whig positions include that of Bernard Mandeville, *The Fable of the Bees*, ed. F. B. Kaye, 2 vols. (Oxford: Oxford University Press, 1966); Lord John Hervey, *Ancient and Modern Liberty, Stated and Compared* (London, 1734); Giles Stephen Holland Fox Strangeways, ed., *Lord John Hervey and His Friends* (London: John Murray, 1950); J. T. Boulton, ed., *Daniel Defoe* (New York: Schocken Books, 1965); and Daniel Defoe, *Moll Flanders*, ed. Juliet Mitchell (Harmondsworth: Penguin Books, 1978). Though Defoe is frequently cited as a champion of commercial modernity, his interpretation of commercial morality was less than sanguine. As Joyce Appleby points out in her essay, "The Social Origins of American Revolutionary Ideology," in *Liberalism, Republicanism in the Historical Imagination* (Cambridge, Mass.: Harvard University Press, 1992), Defoe's response to commerce is illumined by the fact that he sent Moll Flanders to America both to repent of her crimes and to enjoy material success. Morally speaking, however, Moll should have been carted to Tyburn or, like Defoe's Roxana, "the fortunate mistress," endured the "blast of heaven" in unrelieved mental imbalance and distress. See Daniel Defoe, *Roxana, The Fortunate Mistress*, ed. David Blewett (Harmondsworth: Penguin Books, 1987), 379; Manuel Schonhorn, *Defoe's Politics: Parliament, Power, Kingship, and Robinson Crusoe* (Cambridge: Cambridge University Press, 1991); Thomas Keith Meir, *Defoe and the Defense of Commerce* (Victoria, B.C.: English Literary Studies, University of Victoria, 1987); Laurence Dickey, "Power, Commerce, and Natural Law in Daniel Defoe's Political Writings, 1698–1707," in *A Union for Empire: Political Thought and the British Union of 1707*, ed. John Robertson (Cambridge: Cambridge University Press, 1995). On how hard it is to find confident celebrations of commerce in eighteenth-century Anglo-American philosophy, see J. G. A. Pocock, "Cambridge Paradigms and Scotch Philosophers: A Study of the Relations Between the Civic Humanist Tradition and the Civil Jurisprudential Interpretation of Eighteenth-Century Social Thought," in *Wealth and Virtue: The Shaping of Political Economy in the Scottish Enlightenment*, ed. Istvan Hont and Michael Ignatieff (Cambridge: Cambridge University Press, 1983), 240 (hereafter cited as *WV*).

8. Works within the Country tradition include Henry St. John, Viscount Bolingbroke, *Lord Bolingbroke: Historical Writings*, ed. Isaac Kramnick (Chicago: University of Chicago Press, 1972); *The Works of Lord Bolingbroke*, 4 vols. (London: Frank Cass and Company Limited, 1967); Thomas Gordon and John Trenchard, *Cato's Letters* (New York: Russell and Russell, 1969); G. S. Holmes and W. A. Speck, eds., *The Divided Society: Party and Politics in England 1694–1716* (New York: St. Martin's Press, 1967); Andrew Fletcher, *Selected Writings and Speeches*, ed. David Daisches (Edinburgh: Edinburgh University Press, 1979); Adam Ferguson, *An Essay on the History of Civil Society*, ed. Duncan Forbes (Edinburgh: Edinburgh University Press, 1966); Henry Fielding, *New Essays by Henry Fielding: His Contributions to the Craftsman (1734–1739) and other Early Journalism*, ed. Michael G. Farringdon (Charlottesville: University Press of Virginia, 1989); idem, *The True Patriot and Related Writings*, ed. W. B. Coley (Middletown, Conn.: Wesleyan University Press, 1987); and idem, *An Inquiry into the Causes of the Late Increase of Robbers and Related Writings*, ed. Malvin R. Zirker (Middletown, Conn.: Wesleyan University Press, 1988). John Millar repeats some of the arguments made by Country writers in "The Origins of the Distinctions of Ranks," in *John Millar of Glasgow*, ed. W. C. Lehmann (Cambridge: Cambridge University Press, 1960). Millar, however, seems to move beyond

Country politics in his commentary on the relationship between commercialization and democratic government.

9. Studies of the Court-Country debate and its aftermath include: Isaac Kramnick, *Bolingbroke and His Circle: The Politics of Nostalgia in the Age of Walpole* (Cambridge, Mass.: Harvard University Press, 1968); Dennis Rubini, *Court and Country, 1688–1702* (London: Rupert Hart-Davis, 1967); H. T. Dickinson, *Liberty and Property: Political Ideology in Eighteenth-Century Britain* (London: Weidenfeld and Nicholson, 1977); idem, *Walpole and the Whig Supremacy* (London: English Universities Press, 1973); J. A. W. Gunn, *Beyond Liberty and Property: The Process of Self-Recognition in Eighteenth-Century Political Thought* (Kingston: McGill-Queen's University Press, 1983); Quentin Skinner, "The Principles and Practice of Opposition: The Case of Bolingbroke verses Walpole," in *Historical Perspectives*, ed. McKendrick; J. G. A. Pocock, "The Varieties of Whiggism from Exclusion to Reform," *WV*, 235–52; and Richard K. Matthews, ed., *Virtue, Corruption, and Self-Interest: Political Values in the Eighteenth Century* (Bethlehem, Pa.: Lehigh University Press, 1994). Reed Browning reads Court Whiggism as a Ciceronian ideology in his *The Constitutional Ideas of the Court Whigs* (Baton Rouge: Louisiana State University Press, 1982). Shelly Burtt challenges conventional accounts of the role of civic virtue in the Court-Country conflict in her *Virtue Transformed: Political Argument in England, 1688–1740* (Cambridge: Cambridge University Press, 1992). Linda Colley emphasizes the ideological unity of the Tory party and, therefore, criticizes the Court-Country divide as a misleading approach to the period of the Whig ascendancy in her *In Defiance of Oligarchy: The Tory Party, 1714–60* (Cambridge: Cambridge University Press, 1982).

10. See Nicholas Phillipson, "Adam Smith as Civic Moralist," *WV*, 179–202; John Robertson, "Scottish Political Economy at the Limits of the Civic Tradition," *WV*, 137–78; idem, "Scottish Political Economy Beyond the Civic Tradition: Government and Economic Development in the *Wealth of Nations*," *History of Political Thought* 4, no. 3 (winter 1983): 451–82; Donald Winch, *Adam Smith's Politics: An Essay in Historiographic Revision* (Cambridge: Cambridge University Press, 1978); idem, "Adam Smith's Enduring Particular Result," *WV*, 253–69; idem, *Riches and Poverty: An Intellectual History of Political Economy in Britain, 1750–1834* (Cambridge: Cambridge University Press, 1996); and John Berry, *The Idea of Luxury: A Conceptual and Historical Investigation* (Cambridge: Cambridge University Press, 1994).

11. See John Robertson, "Scottish Political Economy At the Limits of the Civic Tradition," *WV*, 137–78. Robertson's approach has much in common with the tack taken by Richard Vetterli and Gary Bryner, *In Search of the Republic: Public Virtue and the Roots of American Government* (Totowa, N.J.: Rowman and Littlefield, 1987). See also Pocock, "Cambridge Paradigms and Scotch Philosophers," 235–52.

12. See Nicholas Phillipson, "Adam Smith as Civic Moralist," *WV*, 179–202; Donald Winch, *Adam Smith's Politics* (Cambridge: Cambridge University Press, 1978); and idem, "Adam Smith's Enduring Particular Result," *WV*, 253–69.

13. See John Robertson, "Scottish Political Economy Beyond the Civic Tradition: Government and Economic Development in the *Wealth of Nations*," *History of Political Thought* 4, no. 3 (winter 1983): 451–82; and John Dwyer, "Virtue and Improvement: the Civic World of Adam Smith," *Adam Smith Reviewed*, ed. Peter Jones and Andrew Skinner (Edinburgh: Edinburgh University Press, 1992), 190–217.

14. See Pocock, "Cambridge Paradigms and Scotch Philosophers," 235–52.

15. Hume, "Of the Parties of Great Britain," in *Essays Moral, Political, and Literary*, ed. Eugene Miller (Indianapolis: Liberty Classics, 1987), 72 (hereafter cited as *Essays*).

16. The striking similarities between Country and Court preoccupations with crime as both a symptom of commercial immorality and a threat to aristocratic identity are apparent in Henry

Fielding, *The Life of Mr. Jonathan Wild, the Great* (Harmondsworth: Penguin Classics, 1982), ed. David Nokes, which contains Daniel Defoe's "True and Genuine Account of the Life and Actions of the Late Jonathan Wild" (229–56). On Jonathan Wild as a representation of Robert Walpole or Walpole as a symbol of Wild, see Nokes's introduction to *The Life of Mr. Jonathan Wild, the Great*; also John Gay, *The Beggar's Opera*, ed. Bryan Loughrey and T. O. Treadwell (Harmondsworth: Penguin Classics, 1986); Fielding, *An Inquiry into the Causes of the Late Increase of Robbers and Related Writings*; and Bernard Mandeville, *An Inquiry into the frequent Executions at Tyburn; and a Proposal for some Regulations concerning Felons in Prison, and the Good Effects to be expected from them*, ed. Malvin R. Zirker (Los Angeles: Augustan Reprint Society, 1964).

Secondary works on this topic include Douglas Hay, ed., *Albion's Fatal Tree: Crime and Society in Eighteenth-Century England* (London: A. Lane Publishers, 1975); John Langbein, "Albion's Fatal Flaws," *Past and Present* 98 (1983); J. S. Cockburn, ed., *Crime in England, 1500–1800* (Cambridge: Cambridge University Press, 1977); John Beattie, "London Crime and the Making of the 'Bloody Code,' 1689–1718"; and Nicholas Rogers, "Confronting the Crime Wave: The Debate over Social Reform and Regulation, 1749–1753," in *Stilling the Grumbling Hive*, ed. Davidson, Hitchcock, Keirn, and Shoemaker. Peter Linebaugh might have made a grand contribution to our understanding of the relationships between criminal activity and social identity in his *The London Hanged: Crime and Civil Society in the Eighteenth Century* (Cambridge: Cambridge University Press, 1992). Unfortunately, Linebaugh's argument is submerged in a swamp of grammatical errors.

17. Smith's affinity with Country ideology stands out in Mary Wollstonecraft's explicit interpretation of the *Wealth of Nations* as an effort to underscore the morally debilitating consequences of commercial progress. In contrast to the way present-day readers tend to set Smith's optimistic opening remarks on the division of labor against his extremely pessimistic comments on specialization near the close of the *Wealth of Nations*, Wollstonecraft compressed both sides of his argument into a unified critique of commercial aristocracy. According to Wollstonecraft,

> The destructive influence of commerce, carried on by men who are eager by overgrown riches to partake of the respect paid to nobility, is felt in a variety of ways. The most pernicious, perhaps, is its producing an aristocracy of wealth, which degrades mankind, by making them only exchange savageness for tame servility, instead of acquiring the urbanity of improved reason. Commerce also, overstocking a country with people, obliges the majority to become manufacturers rather than husbandmen; and then the division of labor, solely to enrich the proprietor, renders the mind entirely inactive. The time which, a celebrated writer says, is sauntered away in going from one employment to another, is the very time that preserves the man from degenerating into a brute . . . thus are whole knots of men turned into machines, to enable a keen speculator to become wealthy; and every noble principle of nature is eradicated by making a man pass his life in stretching wire, pointing a pin, heading a nail, or spreading a sheet of paper on a plain surface.

"An Historical and Moral View of the Origin and Progress of the French Revolution and the Effect It Has Produced in Europe," in *A Wollstonecraft Anthology*, ed. Janet M. Todd (Indiana University Press: 1977), 140. Wollstonecraft clearly did not experience any of the various "Adam Smith Problems" that have plagued so many of his readers. The way Smith appeared in her writings as an unproblematic authority on commercial corruption shows how he was regarded before he was obliged to play the role of apologist or vindicator in the history of political thought. For a reexamination of the traditional "Adam Smith Problem," see Laurence Dickey, "Historicizing the Adam Smith Problem: Conceptual, Historiographical, and Textual Issues," *Journal of Modern History* 58, no. 3 (1986): 579–609. Against Dickey's effort to divide Smith's work into discrete "motivating centers," I would argue much more vaguely that Smith's vision darkened over time. For an inkhorn refutation of Dickey's thesis, see D. D. Raphael, "Adam Smith 1790: The Man Recalled, the Philosopher Revived," in *Adam Smith Reviewed*, ed. Peter Jones and Andrew Skinner (Edinburgh: Edinburgh University Press, 1992).

18. I am clearly following the example set by Donald Winch in his *Adam Smith's Politics*, but I am also trying to provide a historically specific explanation for Smith's commitment to limited government.

19. For example, against John Robertson's contention that Hume managed to reconcile the pursuit of private interest with political capacity, I would emphasize the way Hume dismissed such highflying hopes as destabilizing novelties. See Robertson, "Scottish Political Economy at the Limits of the Civic Tradition," *WV*, 137–78. Likewise, against Nicholas Phillipson's effort to portray Adam Smith as a "civic moralist," I would point out that Smith's main concern was to identify the "vulgar and obvious" principles of human behavior, a project which, he admitted, obliged him to come to conclusions which were "scarce agreeable to good morals or even to good language"; his purpose, in other words, was not to instruct the "wise and virtuous few," the "small party" who studied wisdom and practiced virtue, but to make sense of the corrupting inclinations of the "great mob of mankind" (*TMS*, 61). See Nicholas Phillipson, "Adam Smith as Civic Moralist," *WV*, 179–202.

20. J. G. A. Pocock, "1776: The Revolution Against Parliament," in *Three British Revolutions*, ed. J. G. A. Pocock (Princeton: Princeton University Press, 1976), 279.

21. Pocock, "Cambridge Paradigms and Scotch Philosophers," 243.

22. Ian Shapiro addresses the reductionist tendencies of some recent literature on republicanism in "Pocock's Republicanism," *Critical Review* 4, no. 3 (summer 1990), 433–62. Against Pocock's habit of erasing the passing of centuries in order to identify persistently antibourgeois values, Shapiro points out that, in present-day polemics against the corrupt and criminal practices of popular political leaders such as Ronald Reagan, "it is the undermining of market mechanisms rather than their existence that is held to be at fault" (457).

Without contradicting any of Shapiro's conclusions about Pocock's preoccupation with the persistence of civic humanism, I think that the problem with searching everywhere for echoes of classical republicanism is that the procedure obscures the otherwise obvious role of popular social movements in the transformation of political discourse. The question asked, after all, in republican political theory was not, How might politics be arranged to include a greater portion of the population?, a question that—however outmoded it might sound now, used to animate discussions of democracy—but, How might the population be changed so that some portion of it would be able to cultivate the moral superiority required to participate effectively in political affairs? David Wooton sketches some of the historical and philosophical defects of Pocock's perspective, especially its exclusion of figures such as Tom Paine, in his introduction to his *Republicanism, Liberty, and Commercial Society, 1649–1776*, ed. David Wooten (Stanford: Stanford University Press, 1994).

23. See *WN*, vol. 2, book V, p. 689.

24. See David Cannadine, *The Decline and Fall of the British Aristocracy* (New Haven: Yale University Press, 1990); idem, *Aspects of Aristocracy: Grandeur and Decline in Modern Britain* (New Haven: Yale University Press, 1994); Linda Colley, *Britons: Forging the Nation, 1707–1837* (New Haven: Yale University Press, 1992); Roy Porter, "Georgian Britain: An Ancien Regime?" *British Journal of Eighteenth-Century Studies* 15 (1992): 141–44.

The commercialization of the British aristocracy is one of the major themes in: *Consumption and Culture in the Seventeenth and Eighteenth Centuries*, a three-volume series of essays by an extremely wide range of scholars; *Early Modern Conceptions of Property*, ed. John Brewer and Susan Staves (New York: Routledge, 1995); *Consumption and the World of Goods*, ed. John Brewer and Roy Porter (New York: Routledge, 1993); and *The Consumption of Culture*, ed. Ann Bermingham and John Brewer (New York: Routledge, 1995).

25. Cannadine, *Aspects of Aristocracy*, 33.

26. See David Hume, "Of the Independency of Parliament," *Essays*, 42.

27. *WN*, vol. 1, book I, p. 22.

28. See David McNally, *Political Economy and the Rise of Capitalism* (Berkeley and Los Angeles: University of California Press, 1988); John Dwyer, "Virtue and Improvement: The Civic World of Adam Smith," in *Adam Smith Reviewed*, ed. Peter Jones and Andrew Skinner (Edinburgh: Edinburgh University Press, 1992); Laurence Dickey, "Smith's Critique of Mercantilism and the Problems of the 'Automatic Mechanism' and Agricultural Investment," in *Adam Smith, An Inquiry*, 227–42. Donald Winch addresses various readings of the disappearance of politics in Smith's writings in his *Adam Smith's Politics* (Cambridge: Cambridge University Press, 1978).

29. See Cropsey, *Polity and Economy*; Sheldon Wolin, *Politics and Vision* (Boston: Little Brown, 1960); and Peter Minowitz, *Profits, Priests, and Princes: Adam Smith's Emancipation of Economics from Politics and Religion* (Stanford: Stanford University Press, 1993).

30. See Michael Sandel, "The State and the Soul," *New Republic*, June 10, 1985, 39–42. Don Herzog comments on Sandel's viewpoint in his "Some Questions for Republicans," *Political Theory* 14, no. 3 (August 1986): 473–93. On the historical relevance of republicanism in American politics, see Daniel T. Rogers, "Republicanism: the Career of a Concept," *Journal of Modern History* 79 (June 1992): 11–38. This topic is debated in a special issue of the *Yale Law Review* 97, no. 8 (July 1988). Shelley Burtt reviews some of the same literature in her exploration of the historical vitality and moral flexibility of the republican tradition in her *Virtue Transformed: Political Argument in England, 1688–1740* (Cambridge: Cambridge University Press, 1992).

31. See John Dunn, *The Economic Limits to Modern Politics*, ed. John Dunn (Cambridge: Cambridge University Press, 1990). In his introduction to this volume, Dunn characterizes the distance between political theory and everyday politics as a division between "elite" and "popular" approaches to political life (12). Surely, "marginal" or "insignificant" would be more democratically accurate than "elite." Compare Dunn's standpoint to Smith's observations on the effects of the division of labor in the second chapter of the *Wealth of Nations*:

> The difference between the most dissimilar characters, between a philosopher and a common street porter, for example, seems to arise not so much from nature, as from habit, custom, and education . . . for the first six or eight years of their existence, they were, perhaps, very much alike, and neither their parents nor play-fellows could perceive any remarkable difference. About that age, or soon after, they come to be employed in very different occupations. The difference of talents then . . . widens by degrees, till at last the vanity of the philosopher is willing to acknowledge scarce any resemblance. (*WN*, vol. 1, book I, pp. 28–29)

Though I am kidding, I am kidding because I do not see why studying political theory should be any more significant than working at the Post Office, especially when it can be as pleasurable as writing a novel or spending a day at the beach.

Dunn makes a more determined effort to supply scholarship on the history of political ideas with a heroic dimension in his "The History of Political Theory," in *The History of*

Political Theory and Other Essays (Cambridge: Cambridge University Press, 1996). Grammatical errors make his argument somewhat confusing, but he seems to want his readers to recognize the moral and intellectual superiority of the subject to which he has devoted himself. He argues, for example, that the "great historical texts of political theory" deserve to "command . . . modern attention," both because many of these works offer us special insight into "political causality" and because the traditional canon remains "the carrier of the deepest and most politically intelligent probing of the place of human values within the historical reality of politics" (31). In line with this hierarchical view of political understanding, Dunn insists that "it is both intellectually inept and humanly profligate to an unforgivable degree to view the canon of the history of political theory just as an impressive (or sinister) cultural fossil or an occasion for narcissistic chauvinism" (34).

As a counter to Dunn's celebration of the history of political theory as a fountain of ideas about "collective self-rule," "the human good," and "human values," it seems logical to keep in mind that almost all of the "great historical texts" of the Western tradition can be accurately described as efforts to explain why most people lack the moral competence required to participate in politics. If we remember this definitive aspect of the canon, we can see that it is an exercise in "narcissistic chauvinism" to ignore the fossilized framework of just about all of the "great historical texts." Thus, against the notion that the classics of the Western political tradition ought to be consulted as sources of practical political wisdom, I cite a comment one of my students once made after reading Aristotle: "He's okay if you just leave out the stuff about women and slaves."

John Gunnell complains about the marginality of present-day political theory in his *Between Philosophy and Politics* (Amherst: University of Massachusetts Press, 1986), and in his essay, "Political Science and the Poverty of Theory," in *Through the Looking-Glass: Epistemology and the Conduct of Inquiry*, ed. Maria J. Falco (Washington D.C.: University Press of America, 1979), 92–110. For extended comments on Gunnell's work, see John S. Nelson, ed., *Tradition, Interpretation, and Science: Political Theory in the American Academy* (Albany: State University of New York Press, 1986). Gordon Schochet provides an extremely thoughtful account of the role of political theorists in contemporary society in his "Why Should History Matter? Political Theory and the History of Discourse," in *The Varieties of British Political Thought, 1500–1800*, ed. J. G. A. Pocock, Gordon J. Schochet, and Lois G. Schwoerer (Cambridge: Cambridge University Press, 1993), esp. 346–48.

32. Athol Fitzgibbons stresses Smith's apparent irrelevance to present-day economic theory in *Adam Smith's System of Liberty, Wealth, and Virtue: The Moral and Political Foundations of the Wealth of Nations* (Oxford: Clarendon Press, 1995). Despite his own observations, Fitzgibbons imagines that "a resurgence of interest" in Smith's writings might foster "a new moral liberalism, which this time accepts the weight of human responsibility and dispenses with the mythical paraphernalia of the invisible hand" (194). Having taken up this line of work, I think it would be truly wonderful if Adam Smith scholarship somehow inspired a new and powerful social philosophy. There is, however, simply no reason to suppose that historians of political theory could ever manage, to paraphrase one of Smith's remarks on Mandeville, "to make so much noise in the world."

Chapter 2

1. Bernard Mandeville, *A Treatise of the Hypocrondriak and Hysterick Passions; vulgarly call'd the Hypo in Men and the Vapours in Women*, ed. Stephen H. Good (Delmar, N.Y.: Scholars' Facsimiles and Reprints, 1976). The first edition was published under this title in 1711;

when it was reissued, the title was changed to *A Treatise of the Hypochondriack and Hysterick Diseases* (London: J. Tonson, 1730).

2. Bernard Mandeville, *The Fable of the Bees*, ed. F. B. Kaye, 2 vols. (Oxford: Oxford University Press, 1966), 5 (hereafter cited as *Fable*).

3. See John Carswell, *The South Sea Bubble* (Stanford: Stanford University Press, 1960); Jeremy Black, *Robert Walpole and the Nature of Politics in Early Eighteenth-Century Britain* (New York: St. Martin's Press, 1990); Jeremy Black, ed., *Britain in the Age of Walpole* (New York: St. Martin's Press, 1984); and Charles Mackay, *Memoirs of Extraordinary Popular Delusions and the Madness of Crowds* (London: Richard Bentley, 1841).

4. See Isaac Kramnick, *Bolingbroke and His Circle*, 74; and J. A. W. Gunn, *Beyond Liberty and Property: The Process of Self-Recognition in Eighteenth-Century Political Thought* (Kingston, Ont.: McGill-Queen's University Press, 1983), 106. W. A. Speck portrays Mandeville as a champion of modern Whiggism in "Mandeville and the Eutopia Seated in the Brain," and H. T. Dickinson takes a similar but somewhat more qualified position in his "The Politics of Bernard Mandeville," both in *Mandeville Studies: New Explorations in the Art and Thought of Dr. Bernard Mandeville*, ed. Irwin Primer (The Hague: Martinus Nijhoff, 1975).

5. Mandeville, "Free Thoughts on Religion," quoted in M. M. Goldsmith, *Private Vices and Public Benefits: Bernard Mandeville's Social and Political Thought* (Cambridge: Cambridge University Press, 1985), 99.

6. [Matthew Tindal?], *Our Present Happy Establishment; And the Administration Vindicated*, quoted in Reed Browning, *Political and Constitutional Ideas of the Court Whigs* (Baton Rouge: Louisiana State University Press, 1982), 177.

7. Lord John Hervey, *Lord John Hervey and His Friends*, ed. Giles Stephen Holland Fox-Strangeways, Earl of Illchester (London: John Murray, 1950), 64.

8. Ibid., 41. Hervey presented a much more vigorous defense of modern Whiggism in his *Ancient and Modern Liberty Stated and Compar'd* (1734), ed. H. T. Dickinson (Los Angeles: William Clark Memorial Library, 1985).

9. It is interesting to note how the roles Mandeville assigned to frugality and prodigality are, if not exactly reversed, then at least shifted in Smith's work. Whereas Mandeville suggested that too much frugality would undermine social progress, Smith cited prodigal spending as a formidable threat to general prosperity. Nevertheless, despite Smith's positive conception of frugal conduct, it would be too much to say that he entirely rejected Mandeville's insight into the social benefits of improvidence. Instead, in line with his preoccupation with our natural tendency to pay homage to wealth and greatness, he recognized that, in spite its wasteful results, profligate conduct cements social order. The prodigal habits of the highest ranks give frugality a purpose, not a practical objective, but an ideal goal.

10. In *Beyond Liberty and Property*, Gunn suggests that Mandeville's concept of the "skilful Politician" was designed to flatter the Whigs (102–3).

11. On the problems involved in any literal interpretation of Mandeville's observations on "those who would civilize mankind," see Goldsmith, *Private Vices, Public Benefits* (61–77). Goldsmith argues that Mandeville's concept of the "skilful Politician" was supposed to represent the accumulated knowledge of society itself.

12. Mandeville, "Free Thoughts on Religion," quoted in Goldsmith, *Private Vices, Public Benefits*, 95.

13. Jacob Viner addresses Mandeville's mercantilism in his "Introduction to Mandeville," in *Essays on the Intellectual History of Economics* (Princeton: Princeton University Press, 1991). Like E. G. Hundert, in his *The Enlightenment's Fable: Bernard Mandeville and the Discovery of Society* (Cambridge: Cambridge University Press, 1994), Viner points out that efforts to raise

Mandeville's observations on economic prosperity to the level of systematic theory generally tend to exaggerate his role in the making of classical political economy.

14. See Thomas A. Horne, *The Social Thought of Bernard Mandeville* (New York: Columbia University Press, 1978), 68–73. Hector Monro addresses this point in The *Ambivalence of Bernard Mandeville* (Oxford: Oxford University Press, 1975). In keeping with the title of his book, Monro does not lay it to rest.

15. E. G. Hundert explores this point in his chapter on "Performance Principles in the Public Sphere" in his *The Enlightenment's Fable: Bernard Mandeville and the Discovery of Society* (Cambridge: Cambridge University Press, 1994).

16. See Albert O. Hirschman, *The Passions and the Interests: Political Arguments for Capitalism Before Its Triumph* (Princeton University Press, 1977).

17. See Henry Fielding, *Johnathan Wild*, ed. David Nokes (London: Penguin Classics, 1982); idem, *Joseph Andrews* (New York: Signet Classics, 1960); idem, *New Essays by Henry Fielding: His Contributions to the Craftsman and Other Early Journalism (1734–1739)*, ed. Michael C. Farringdon (Charlottesville: University of Virginia Press, 1989); John Gay, *The Beggar's Opera*, ed. Bryan Loughrey and T. O. Treadwell (Harmondsworth: Penguin Classics, 1986); and Alexander Pope, "The Dunciad," and "Of the Use of Riches," in *Pope's Dunciad of 1728: A History and Facsimile*, ed. David L. Vander Meulen (Charlottesville: University Press of Virginia, 1991).

18. Henry Fielding, "An Inquiry in the Causes of the Late Increase of Robbers," in *An Inquiry in the Causes of the Late Increase of Robbers and Related Writings*, ed. Malvin R. Zirker (Middletown, Conn.: Wesleyan University Press, 1988), 77.

19. Bolingbroke, "A Dissertation Upon Parties," *Works*, 1:165; David Hume, *An Inquiry into the Principles of Morals*, ed. Charles W. Hendel (Indianapolis: Bobbs-Merrill, 1957), 103; and Smith, *WN*, vol. 2, book V, p. 794.

20. Hundert, *The Enlightenment's Fable*, 60–61.

21. M. M. Goldsmith discusses the Scottish response to the *Fable of the Bees* in "Regulating Anew the Moral and Political Sentiments of Mankind: Bernard Mandeville and the Scottish Enlightenment," *Journal of the History of Ideas* 49 (October–December 1988), 587–606.

Chapter 3

1. This chapter owes a great deal to Kramnick, *Bolingbroke and His Circle*. Other sources include Jeremy Black, ed., *Britain in the Age of Walpole* (New York, St. Martin's Press, 1984); W. A. Speck, *Stability and Strife: England, 1714–1760* (Cambridge: Harvard University Press, 1977); John Cannon, ed. *The Whig Ascendancy: Colloquies on Hanoverian England* (London: Edward Arnold, 1981); H. T. Dickinson, *Walpole and the Whig Supremacy* (London: English Universities Press, 1973); McKendrick, ed., *Historical Perspectives*; Bertrand A. Goldgar, *Walpole and the Wits: The Relation of Politics to Literature, 1722–1742* (Omaha: University of Nebraska Press, 1976.); J. A. W. Gunn, *Beyond Liberty and Property: The Process of Self-Recognition in Eighteenth-Century Political Thought* (Kingston: McGill-Queen's University Press, 1971; idem, *Politics and the Public Interest in the Seventeenth Century* (London: Routledge, Kegan Paul, 1969; and J. R. Jones, ed., *Liberty Secured?: Britain Before and After 1688* (Stanford: Stanford University Press, 1992).

2. A paraphrase of Bolingbroke's definition of history as "philosophy teaching by examples"; see Bolingbroke, "Letters on the Study and Use of History," in *Lord Bolingbroke: Historical Writings*, ed. Issac Kramnick (Chicago: University of Chicago Press, 1972), 9.

3. Bolingbroke, "The Idea of a Patriot King," *The Works of Lord Bolingbroke*, 4 vols. (London: Frank Cass and Company Limited, 1967), 2:374 (hereafter cited as *Works*).

4. Bolingbroke, quoted in Kramnick, *Bolingbroke and His Circle*, 74.

5. Bolingbroke, "A Dissertation upon Parties," *Works*, 2:150–51.

6. Bolingbroke, "On the Power of the Prince," *Works*, 1:510.

7. Bolingbroke, *Contributions to the Craftsman*, ed. Simon Varey (Oxford: Clarendon Press, 1982), no. 377, 22 September 1733, p. 166 (hereafter cited as *Craftsman*).

8. Ibid., 162.

9. Bolingbroke, *Craftsman*, no. 406, 13 April 1734, p. 170.

10. See J. G. A. Pocock, *The Machiavellian Moment: Florentine Political Thought and the Atlantic Republican Tradition* (Princeton: Princeton University Press, 1975).

11. Bolingbroke, "On the Power of the Prince," *Works*, 1:510.

12. See Lord John Hervey, *Ancient and Modern Liberty, Stated and Compared* (London, 1724); Reed Browning, *The Political and Constitutional Ideas of the Court Whigs* (Baton Rouge: Louisiana State University Press, 1980); and J. G. A. Pocock, *The Ancient Constitution and the Feudal Law* (Cambridge: Cambridge University Press, 1987), 335–87.

13. I believe that the phrase "starve liberty by neglect" appears somewhere in the pre-revolutionary pamphlets explored in: Gordon Wood, *The Creation of the American Republic* (Chapel Hill: University of North Carolina Press, 1969); idem, *The Radicalism of the American Revolution* (New York: Alfred A. Knopf, 1992); or Bernard Bailyn, *The Ideological Origins of the American Revolution* (Cambridge, Mass.: Harvard University Press, 1967. To some extent, this chapter is designed to counter Quentin Skinner's view of Bolingbroke as a purely strategic thinker in his "The Principles and Practice of Opposition: The Case of Bolingbroke vs. Walpole," in *Historical Perspectives*, ed. Neil McKendrick. Without suggesting that Bolingbroke was an entirely honest writer, I think that the notion that he "deployed" certain arguments simply to score points against his opponents obscures the emotional content of his work.

14. Bolingbroke, "Dissertation Upon on Parties," *Works*, 2:86.

15. Ibid., 2:94.

16. Bolingbroke, "On the Spirit of Patriotism," *Works*, 2:354, 355. In the *Craftsman*, Bolingbroke recited the resume of a decent member of Parliament in a more restrained fashion. Among the "the Marks of a good Parliament-man," he included "Riches with Frugality; Integrity; Courage; being well-affected to the Constitution; Knowledge of the State of the Country; being prudently frugal of the Money; careful of the Trade; having stuck to the Interests of his Country in Perilous Times; and being assiduous in Attendance" (no. 377, 22 September 1733, p. 167).

17. Bolingbroke, *Craftsman*, no. 111, 17 August 1728, p. 52.

18. Bolingbroke, "A Dissertation Upon Parties," *Works*, 2:65.

19. Ibid., 2:164–65. After reading an earlier version of this chapter, Isaac Kramnick kindly advised me to avoid archaic terms such as "newfangled." But since I wouldn't mind cruising in a souped-up jalopy, I could not take his advice.

20. Ibid., 2:165.

21. Bolingbroke, "Remarks on the History of England," *Works*, 1:376. Compare Madison, "Liberty is to faction what air is to fire, an aliment without which it instantly expires" (James Madison, *The Federalist Papers*, no. 10, ed. Clinton Rossiter [New York: New American Library, 1961], 78). See also Douglas Adair, *Fame and the Founding Fathers* (Williamsburg: Institute for Early American History and Culture, 1974). Madison's simile contrasts with Bolingbroke's declaration in "Remarks on the History of England": "But it will remain eternally true that

the spirit of liberty and the spirit of faction are not only different, but repugnant and incompatible: so that the life of either is the death of the other" (*Works*, 1:305).

22. Bolingbroke, *Craftsman*, no. 130, 28 December 1728, p. 63.

23. Ibid., no. 114, 7 September 1728, p. 58.

24. Bolingbroke, "The Idea of a Patriot King," *Works*, 2:375.

25. See Kramnick, *Bolingbroke and His Circle*, 166–67; Kramnick refers to J. G. A. Pocock, *The Ancient Constitution and the Feudal Law: English Historical Thought in the Seventeenth Century* (New York: W. W. Norton, 1967), 146–47.

26. Bolingbroke, "Remarks on the History of England," *Works*, 2:369, 393.

27. Bolingbroke, *Craftsman*, no. 406, 13 April 1734, p. 172.

28. Bolingbroke, "On the Spirit of Patriotism," *Works*, 2:363.

29. Ibid., 111.

30. See J. H. Plumb, *The Origins of Political Stability in England, 1675–1725* (Boston: Houghton Mifflin Company, 1967).

Chapter 4

1. David Hume, "A Character of Sir David Hume, "A Character of Sir Robert Walpole," in *Essays*, 575–76. This piece first appeared in 1742, just before Walpole's removal. In later editions, it was appended as a footnote to "May Politics Be Reduced A Science." In those editions, Hume added a note to the note which identified the public debt as a "great, and the only great, error in that long administration." This chapter draws a great deal from Duncan Forbes, *Hume's Philosophical Politics* (Cambridge: Cambridge University Press, 1978); and J. G. A. Pocock, "Hume and the American Revolution: The Dying Thoughts of a North Briton," in his *Virtue, Commerce, and History*, 125–42.

2. Hume, "The Rise of Arts and Sciences," *Essays*, 113.

3. Hume, "Of Public Credit," *Essays*, 352.

4. Ibid., 351.

5. *WN*, 1:265.

6. Hume, "Of Public Credit," *Essays*, 359.

7. Ibid., 358.

8. Ibid., 365.

9. Hume, "Of Refinement of the Arts," *Essays*, 271.

10. Hume, "Of Commerce," *Essays*, 262–63.

11. See, in particular, John Robertson, "The Scottish Enlightenment at the Limits of the Civic Tradition," in *WV*, 137–78; and "Scottish Political Economy Beyond the Civic Tradition: Government and Economic Development in the *Wealth of Nations*," *History of Political Thought* 4 (winter 1983), 451–82. Joyce Appleby takes a somewhat similar view of the relationship between the republican and liberal traditions in her *Capitalism and a New Social Order: The Republican Vision of the 1790's* (New York: New York University Press, 1984). See also Joyce Appleby, *Liberalism and Republicanism in the Historical Imagination* (Cambridge, Mass.: Harvard University Press, 1992).

12. Hume, "Of the Origin of Justice and Property," *A Treatise of Human Nature*, Book 3, *Hume's Moral and Political Philosophy*, ed. Henry D. Aiken (New York: Hafner Publishing Company, 1948), 61 (hereafter cited as *Treatise*). Hume's arguments on the plain necessity for justice have much in common with Smith's observations on the same subject.

According to Smith,

But though it commonly requires no great discernment to see the destructive tendency of all licentious practices to the welfare of society, it is seldom this consideration that first animates us against them. All men, even the most stupid and unthinking, abhor fraud, perfidy, and injustice, and delight to see them punished. But few men have reflected upon the necessity of justice to the existence of society, how obvious soever that necessity may appear to be. (*TMS*, 89)

13. *Treatise*, 62.

14. Hume, "Origin of Government," *Essays*, 34.

15. Ibid., 38

16. Ibid., 39.

17. Hume, "Of the Original Contract," *Essays*, 474.

18. Ibid., 473.

19. Hume, "Of the Independency of Parliament," *Essays*, 42.

20. Hume, "That Politics May Be Reduced to a Science," *Essays*, 24.

21. Hume, "Independency of Parliament," *Essays*, 45.

22. Hume, "Of the Parties of Great Britain," *Essays*, 72.

23. Hume, "Politics A Science," *Essays*, 28–29.

24. Hume, "Whether the British Government Inclines More to Absolute Monarchy, or to a Republic," *Essays*, 49–50.

25. Ibid., 53.

26. In his conclusion to "Of the Original Contract," Hume wrote: "The only passage I meet with in antiquity, where the obligation of obedience to government is ascribed to a promise, is in Plato's *Crito*: where SOCRATES refuses to escape from prison, because he had tacitly promised to obey the laws. Thus he builds a tory consequence of passive obedience on a whig foundation of the original contract" (*Essays*, 487).

27. *Treatise*, 14.

28. Hume, "Of the Coalition of Parties," *Essays*, 495.

29. I have a feeling that this phrase might have appeared in something I have read, but I cannot remember where and cannot bear to give it up.

30. Hume, "Of the Coalition of Parties," *Essays*, 496.

31. Ibid., 501.

32. Ibid., 500.

33. See Kramnick, *Bolingbroke and His Circle*, 82.

34. Hume, "My Own Life," *Essays*, xxxviii. Of the revisions he made to his *History of England*, Hume wrote:

But though I had been taught by experience that the Whig Party were in possession of bestowing all places, both in the state and in literature, I was so little inclined to yield to their senseless clamor, that in above a hundred alterations, which farther study, reading or reflection engaged me to make in the reigns of the first two Stuarts, I have made all of them invariably on the Tory side. It is ridiculous to consider the English constitution before that period as a regular plan of liberty. (Ibid.)

His reference to the Tories appears at the close of "The Parties of Great Britain" (*Essays*, 72).

35. See Linda Colley, *In Defiance of Oligarchy: The Tory Party, 1714–60* (Cambridge: Cambridge University Press, 1982).

Chapter 5

1. While Marx might be blamed for promoting Smith's reputation as an apologist, it was, Marx, after all, who, by deriving the skeleton of his critique of capitalism from the *Wealth of Nations*, allowed us to designate Smith as the primary source of both liberal and socialist theory. Smith may not have been nearly as fond of literary fame as Hume declared himself to be, but he might have enjoyed the way his alleged contradictions led him to such an illustrious place in the history of political and economic thought. On Smith as Marx's main inspiration, see Ronald Meek, *Smith, Marx, and After: Ten Essays in the Development of Economic Thought* (New York: Wiley and Sons, 1977).

2. On Smith as a proponent of agrarian capitalism, see David McNally, *Political Economy and the Rise of Capitalism* (Berkeley and Los Angeles: University of California Press, 1988). John Dwyer adds a more specifically civic dimension to McNally's thesis in "Virtue and Improvement: the Civic World of Adam Smith," *Adam Smith Reviewed*, ed. Peter Jones and Andrew Skinner (Edinburgh: Edinburgh University Press, 1992). On Smith as a vindicator of Whig aristocracy, see Pocock, "Cambridge Paradigms and Scotch Philosophers," 235–52. John Robertson interprets Smith as a problem-solver in "Scottish Political Economy Beyond the Civic Tradition: Government and Economic Development in the *Wealth of Nations*," *History of Political Thought* 4, no. 3 (winter 1983): 451–82. Nicholas Phillipson portrays Smith as an advisor to the young men of Scotland in "Adam Smith as Civic Moralist," *WV*, 179–202. On what Smith might have accomplished if he had not died first, see Donald Winch, *Adam Smith's Politics: An Essay in Historiographic Revision* (Cambridge: Cambridge University Press, 1978), esp. 11–27; idem, "Adam Smith's Enduring Particular Result: A Political and Cosmopolitan Perspective," in *WV*, 253–70. Winch also discusses Smith's unfinished work in *Riches and Poverty: An Intellectual History of Political Economy in Britain, 1750–1834* (Cambridge: Cambridge University Press, 1996).

3. See Pocock, "Cambridge Paradigms and Scotch Philosophers," 235–52.

4. *WN*, vol. 1, book II, p. 343.

5. In case it seems that this statement somehow resolves the political problems presented by the pursuit of private interest, it should be remembered that Smith's political system specifically excludes "by far the greater part of mankind."

6. John Rae, quoted in Duncan Forbes, "Skeptical Whiggism, Commerce, and Liberty," *Essays on Adam Smith*, ed. Andrew Skinner and Thomas Wilson (Oxford: Oxford University Press, 1976), 195.

7. Hume, "Of Public Credit," *Essays*, 358.

8. Bolingbroke, "The Idea of a Patriot King," *Works*, 1:165.

9. Bolingbroke, "A Dissertation Upon Parties," *Works*, 1:165.

10. Smith's preoccupation with the unreality of social hierarchy contrasts with Henry Fielding's remarks on the burdens of social responsibility in his "A Modest Proposal for Making an Effectual Provision for the Poor." According to Fielding,

> Those Duties, however, which fall to the higher ranks of Men, even in this Commonwealth, are by no means the lightest or easiest kind. The Watchings, the Fatigues, the Anxieties and Cares which attend the highest Stations, render their Possessors, in real Truth, no proper objects of Envy to those in the lowest, whose Labours are much less likely to impair the Health of their Bodies, or to destroy the Peace of their Minds; are not less consistent with their Happiness, and much more consistent with their Safety.

An Inquiry into the Causes of the Late Increase of Robbers and Related Writings, ed. Malvin R. Zirker (Middletown, Conn.: Wesleyan University Press, 1988), 227. For Fielding, in other words, the poor are better off than their superiors because they are free from the anxieties attached to profound obligations; for Smith, the poor are better off because they are relatively protected from the anxieties induced by the deceptions of avarice and ambition.

11. Hume, "Of Public Credit," *Essays*, 358.

12. David Hume, "A Treatise of Human Nature," *Hume's Moral and Political Philosophy*, ed. Henry D. Aiken (New York: Hafner Publishing Company, 1948), 14.

13. *WN*, vol. 1, book I, pp. 28–29.

14. Smith's observations here have much in common with his conclusions in his "The History of Astronomy," in which he suggested that the apparent compass of certain scientific theories, particularly the system of Newtonian philosophy, makes them so attractive to the imagination that we are apt to be indifferent to their actual validity. See Smith, "The History of Astronomy," *Essays on Philosophical Subjects*, ed. W. P. D. Wightman and J. C. Bryce (Indianapolis: Liberty Classics, 1982). Andrew Hemingway pointed this out to me. I am grateful for his insight into this aspect of Smith's philosophy and for his comprehensive understanding of the general ideological framework of the Scottish Enlightenment. Andrew Hemingway, "The 'Sociology' of Taste in the Scottish Enlightenment," *Oxford Art Journal* 12, no. 2 (1989): 3–35.

15. On the problem of individual identity within a competitive society, see Robert L. Heilbroner, *Behind the Veil of Economics: Essays in the Worldly Philosophy* (New York: Norton, 1988). For an approach to this problem that deals more specifically with Smith, see Robert L. Heilbroner, "The Socialization of the Individual in Adam Smith," *History of Political Economy* 14, nos. 3421–31. Robert Urquhart discusses Heilbroner's views of the relationship between individual motivation and economic competition in "Adam Smith Between Political Economy and Economics," in *Economics as a Worldly Philosophy: Essays in Political and Historical Economics in Honour of Robert L. Heilbroner*, ed. Ron Blackwell, Jaspal Chatha, and Edward Nell (New York: St. Martin's Press, 1993).

16. *WN*, vol. 1, book II, pp. 341–42.

17. Ibid., book III, p. 456.

18. The emphasis placed on selfishness here may seem to contradict the doctrine of sympathy set forth in the *Theory of Moral Sentiments*; the best way to lay to rest such contradictions is to recollect the consistently skeptical tone of Smith's work. A paragraph at the start of the *Theory of Moral Sentiments* presents a case in point:

> Howsoever selfish man may be supposed, there are evidently some principles in his nature, which interest him in the fortune of others, and render their happiness necessary to him, though he derives nothing from it except the pleasure of seeing it. . . . That we often derive sorrow from the sorrow of others, is a matter of fact too obvious to require any instances to prove it; for this sentiment, like all the other original passions of human nature, is by no means confined to the virtuous and humane, though they perhaps may feel it with the most exquisite sensibility. The greatest ruffian, the most hardened violator of the laws of society, is not altogether without it. (*TMS*, 9)

In other words, given the "coarse clay of which the bulk of mankind are formed," sympathy stands as an undeniable anomaly, an exception that, since it shows itself even among the lowest and least virtuous members of society, needs to be explained (*TMS*, 163).

19. *WN*, vol. 1, book IV, p. 540.

20. Ibid., book II, p. 346.

21. Ibid., book III, pp. 418–19.

22. Ibid., p. 412.

23. Ibid., p. 422. In "'The Nature of Things' and the Monetarization of History," Laurence Dickey reads Smith's rendition of the demise of feudalism as "an object lesson for what happens to the worldly fortunes of people who, lacking the power of self-command, indulge in the kind of selfish consumption of luxury goods that brought the barons to ruin." See *Adam Smith*, 224–25. Smith's commentary on the social and political improvements inadvertently advanced by the "childish vanity" of the great proprietors was, I think, designed as a comment on the moral limitations of the richest and most powerful members of eighteenth-century British society, but, rather than trying to teach such people about the dangers of indulgence, Smith was trying to show that their intractable stupidity did not prevent them from unknowingly promoting the public good.

24. See John Robertson, "Scottish Political Economy Beyond the Civic Tradition: Government and Economic Development in the *Wealth of Nations*," *History of Political Thought* 4, no. 3 (winter 1983), 451–82. See also Duncan Forbes, "Skeptical Whiggism, Commerce, and Liberty," *Essays on Adam Smith*. Donald Winch reviews the connections various scholars have drawn between commercial progress and political liberty in *Adam Smith's Politics: An Essay in Historiographic Revision* (Cambridge: Cambridge University Press, 1978). Smith's arguments about increasing economic independence and political stability contrast with the political conclusions drawn by his student, John Millar. Whereas Smith emphasized "order and good government" as the unintended consequence of the decline of the great feudal lords, Millar argued:

> It cannot be doubted that these circumstances have a tendency to introduce a democratical government. As persons of inferior rank are placed in a situation which, in point of subsistence, renders them little dependent upon their superiors; as no one order of men continues in the exclusive possession of opulence; and as every man who is industrious may entertain the hope of gaining a fortune; it is to be expected that the prerogatives of the monarch and of the ancient nobility will be gradually undermined; that the privileges of the people will be extended . . . and that power, the usual attendant of wealth, will be in some measure diffused over all the members of the community.

John Millar, "The Origin of the Distinction of Ranks," in *John Millar of Glasgow*, ed. William C. Lehman (Cambridge: Cambridge University Press, 1960), 292. Smith, in keeping with his skeptical view of political authority, stressed the "diffusion of opulence," rather than any diffusion of power.

25. *WN*, vol. 1, book IV, p. 493.

26. Ibid., vol. 2, book IV, p. 687.

27. See Albert O. Hirschman, *The Passions and the Interests: Political Arguments for Capitalism Before Its Triumph* (Princeton University Press, 1977). Hirschman modifies and expands his views on the transition from "passions" to "interests" in *Rival Views of Market Society and Other Recent Essays* (New York: Viking Penguin, 1986). In his earlier book, Hirschman distinguishes his reading of Smith from that of Joseph Cropsey by quoting Cropsey's contention that, generally speaking, "Smith's position may be interpreted to mean that commerce generates freedom and civilization, and at the same time, free institutions are indispensable to the preservation of commerce" (*The Passions and the Interests*, 104).

To the extent that "freedom and civilization" may be viewed as non-political values, Cropsey and Hirschman seem to have a great deal in common. For Cropsey, the outstanding feature of Smith's work is the way it replaced political considerations with economic concerns. Likewise, for Hirschman, the *Wealth of Nations* signifies the end of a long-term effort to legitimize commerce by stressing its political benefits. Along these lines, Hirschman observes, "The main impact of the *Wealth of Nations* was to establish a powerful *economic* justification for the untrammeled pursuit of individual interest, whereas in the earlier literature that has been surveyed here the stress was on the *political* effects of this pursuit (*The Passions and the Interests*, 100). Hirschman qualifies this observation by calling attention to the political "revolution" Smith attributed to the frivolous pursuits of the great proprietors during the decline of feudalism. Smith's point, however, was not that the demise of feudalism opened up any new avenues for political practice or participation, but that the lords had inadvertently strengthened stability of possession by wasting their authority in thoughtless consumption. Given the profound political oblivion Smith identified as the driving force behind this historical "revolution," his chapter on the disintegration of the feudal system could be designated as an "anti-political argument for capitalism before its triumph."

28. *WN*, vol. 1, book I, p. 265.

29. Ibid., 266.

30. Ibid., vol. 2, book V, p. 782.

31. Ibid., vol. 1, I, pp. 266–67.

32. Ibid., book IV, p. 456.

33. Ibid., 471.

34. Ibid., vol. 2, book IV, p. 674.

35. See Duncan Forbes, "Skeptical Whiggism, Commerce, and Liberty," in *Essays on Adam Smith*, ed. Andrew Skinner and Thomas Wilson (Oxford: Oxford University Press, 1976). Joseph Cropsey, "Adam Smith and Political Philosophy," in the same collection. In "Adam Smith," Jacob Viner defined the "individual's choice of occupation, residence, or investment" and "freedom for the individual to make his economic decisions of all kinds in response to the price movements of free and fully competitive markets" as the fundamental freedoms Smith regarded as "natural rights," essential constituents of the dignity of man (Jacob Viner, *Essays on the Intellectual History of Economics* [Princeton: Princeton University Press, 1991], 258).

Against this classic view, I would argue that Smith saw competitive markets as a way to minimize rather than maximize individual choice. After all, Smith valued economic competition only because it promoted frugality and self-discipline. He also stressed that the more protected individuals are from the pressures of competition, the more likely they are to fall into disorderly dissipation. Finally, without denying that Smith regarded property-ownership as a basic right, it is, I think, important not to translate Smith's conception of social and economic freedom into political terms. Anyone who admits that Smith's doctrine of unintended benefits plays an important role in his work must, in short, admit that liberty and oblivion cannot be reconciled.

36. As J. G. A. Pocock observes, "Nature may be developed, but cannot be distributed; you cannot distribute a *telos*, only the means to it; virtue cannot therefore be reduced to matter of right" ("Virtues, Rights, and Manners: A Model for Historians of Political Thought," 358–59; quoted by Ian Shapiro, "Pocock's Republicanism," *Critical Review* 4, no. 3 (summer 1990): 464.

37. *WN*, vol. 2, book V, p. 794.

38. In light of Smith's remarks on the moral superiority of the common people, especially their tendency toward frugality, Laurence Dickey has lately maintained that Smith meant to "charge . . . human beings . . . with the responsibility for retrenching expenses and for ameliorating debilitating social conditions" because he hoped that doing so would promote a "democratization of the habit of frugality" (Laurence Dickey, "*Deux-Commerce* and the 'Mediocrity of Money' Problem," in *Adam Smith, An Inquiry*, 257, 259).

However, except as a way to supply Smith's arguments on frugality with political connotations, the term "democratization" makes no sense. Smith's point was, after all, that frugality is a popular virtue by necessity; that is, the overwhelming majority of people are frugal because they generally have no other choice. Smith accordingly celebrated frugality not because he expected more people to practice that virtue, but because he believed that the largely obligatory parsimony of the many compensates for the prodigality prevalent among the propertied few. John Dwyer examines Smith's views on frugality in his "Virtue and Improvement: the Civic World of Adam Smith," *Adam Smith Reviewed*, ed. Peter Jones and Andrew Skinner (Edinburgh: Edinburgh University Press, 1992).

39. *WN*, vol. 2, book V, p. 794.

40. Ibid., vol. 1, book II, p. 341.

41. Ibid., 342.

42. Ibid., 342–43.

43. Ibid., vol. 2, book V, p. 814.

44. Ibid., 908–9.

45. Ibid., 814.

46. Linda Colley addresses both the unprecedented power the landed elite gained in the course of the eighteenth-century and the problems this success posed to their social and political identity in *Britons: Forging the Nation, 1707–1837*. Mark Girouard addresses the role of the country house in maintaining social inequality in *Life in the English Country House: A Social and Architectural History* (New Haven: Yale University Press, 1978). W. D. Rubenstein stresses the "almost total ascendancy of the landed aristocracy" until the mid-nineteenth century in "Businessmen into Landowners: The Question Revisited," in *Land and Society in Britain*, ed. Harte and Quinault, 115.

47. David Hume, *An Inquiry into the Principles of Morals*, ed. Charles W. Hendel (Indianapolis: Bobbs-Merrill Educational Publishing, 1957), 103.

48. Athol Fitzgibbons seems to argue that Smith envisioned a more democratic society in his *Adam Smith's System of Liberty, Wealth, and Virtue: The Moral and Political Foundations of The Wealth of Nations* (Oxford: Clarendon Press, 1995). For example, Fitzgibbons insists, "Smith especially wanted the lower classes to participate in public life." However, rather than citing any evidence to show that Smith ever entertained such an egalitarian objective, Fitzgibbons first vaguely refers to some "new class" Smith apparently imagined, then proceeds to recite Smith's extremely pessimistic comments on the possibility of competent political leadership (160). This lack of evidence, along with Fitzgibbons' imposition of the terms "left" and "Right" (sometimes capitalized, sometimes not) upon eighteenth-century British moral philosophy, makes his reading of Smith's intentions extremely hard to understand (153, 154).

49. *WN*, vol. 2, book IV, p. 687.

50. Bolingbroke, "The Idea of a Patriot King," *Works*, 2:375.

Postscript

1. Tom Paine, "The Rights of Man," *The Thomas Paine Reader*, ed. Michael Foote and Isaac Kramnick (New York: Viking Penguin, 1987), 277.

2. Thomas Malthus, *An Essay on the Principle of Population*, ed. Donald Winch (Cambridge: Cambridge University Press, 1992), book III, p. 48 (hereafter cited as Malthus).

3. Malthus, book IV, p. 329.

4. Ibid., 245.

5. Ibid., 247–48.

6. Ibid., 250. David Cannadine places Malthus's doctrine of popular privation within the context of aristocratic prosperity in "Conspicuous Consumption by the Landed Classes, 1790–1830," in *Malthus and His Time,* ed. Michael Turner (New York: St. Martin's Press, 1986).

7. Malthus, 315. Malthus's commitment to aristocratic ascendancy is especially apparent in his affinity with Hume. Echoing Hume's complaints about the tumult which would follow if the common people rejected aristocratic authority, Malthus warned,

> Should such periods [of scarcity] often recur, (a recurrence which we have too much reason to apprehend from the present state of the country) . . . the English constitution will be seen hastening with rapid strides to Euthanasia foretold by Hume. . . . If political discontents were blended with cries of hunger, and a revolution were to take place by the instrumentality of a mob clamouring for want of food, the consequences would be unceasing change and unceasing carnage, the bloody career of which nothing but the establishment of some complete despotism could arrest. (Malthus, book IV, p. 245)

8. George Gilder's *Wealth and Poverty* (New York: Basic Books, 1981) presents a fairly representative example of the general argument. For a wider range of ruthless recommendations, see Neal Kozodoy, ed., *What to Do About . . . A Collection of Essays from Commentary Magazine* (New York: Regan Books, 1995); and Mark Gerson, ed., *The Essential Neoconservative Reader* (New York: Addison-Wesley Publishing Company, 1996). Jean Stefanic and Richard Delgado explain how such recommendations gained so much currency in *No Mercy: How Conservative Think Tanks and Foundations Changed America's Social Agenda* (Philadelphia: Temple University Press, 1996). Nicolaus Mills looks at some of the cultural symptoms of this agenda in *The Triumph of Meanness: America's War Against Its Better Self* (Boston and New York: Houghton Mifflin Company, 1997). For an examination of the effects of neocon policies, see Edward N. Wolff, *Top Heavy: A Study of the Increasing Inequality of Wealth in America* (New York: The Twentieth Century Fund, 1995). See also Sheldon Danziger and Peter Gottschalk, eds., *Uneven Tides: Rising Inequality in America* (New York: Russell Sage Foundation, 1993). Joel F. Handler and Yeheskel Hasenfeld explore the social sentiments attached to welfare cuts in *We the Poor People: Work, Poverty, and Welfare* (New Haven and London: Yale University Press, 1997). Barbara Ehrenreich tells a somewhat similar story in *Fear of Falling: The Inner Life of the Middle Class* (New York: HarperCollins, 1990).

9. See John Dunn, ed., *The Economic Limits to Politics* (Cambridge: Cambridge University Press, 1990).

10. See, in particular, James Paul Gee, Glynda Hull, Colin Lankshear, *The New Work Order: Behind the Language of the New Capitalism* (Boulder: Westview Press, 1996); Edward S. Herman, *Triumph of the Market: Essays on Economics, Politics, and the Media* (Boston: South End Press, 1995); John Walton and David Seddon, *Free Markets and Food Riots: The Politics of Global Adjustment* (Cambridge, Mass.: Blackwell Publishers, 1994); and Gosta Esping-Andersen, ed., *Welfare States in Transition: National Adaptations in Global Economies* (London: Sage Publications, 1996). See also the newer edition of Daniel Bell's *The Cultural Contradictions of Capitalism* (New York: Basic Books, 1996); Robert Kuttner, *Everything for Sale: The Virtues and Limits of Markets* (New York: Alfred A. Knopf, 1997); and Ruth Colker, *American Law in the Age of Hypercapitalism: The Worker, the Family, and the State* (New York: New York University Press, 1998).

11. *WN,* vol. 1, book I, p. 266.

BIBLIOGRAPHY

Adair, Douglas. 1974. *Fame and the Founding Fathers*. Williamsburg: Institute for Early American History and Culture.

Agnew, Jean-Christophe. 1986. *Worlds Apart: The Market and the Theater in Anglo-American Thought, 1550–1750*. Cambridge: Cambridge University Press.

Hervey, Lord John. 1985. *Ancient and Modern Liberty Stated and Compar'd* (1734), ed. H. T. Dickinson. Los Angeles: William Clark Memorial Library.

Appleby, Joyce. 1992. *Liberalism and Republicanism in the Historical Imagination*. Cambridge, Mass.: Harvard University Press.

———. 1984. *Capitalism and a New Social Order: The Republican Vision of the 1790's*. New York: New York University Press.

Bailyn, Bernard. 1967. *The Ideological Origins of the American Revolution*. Cambridge, Mass.: Harvard University Press.

Barrel, John. 1992. *The Birth of Pandora and the Division of Knowledge*. Philadelphia: University of Pennsylvania Press.

———. 1986. *The Political Theory of Painting from Reynolds to Hazlitt: The "Body of the Public."* New Haven: Yale University Press.

Baugh, Daniel A., ed. 1975. *Aristocratic Government and Society in Eighteenth-Century England: The Foundations of Stability*. New York: New Viewpoints.

Beier, A. L., David Cannadine, and James M. Rosenheim, eds. 1989. *The First Modern Society: Essays in English History in Honour of Lawrence Stone*. Cambridge: Cambridge University Press.

Bell, Daniel. 1996. *The Cultural Contradictions of Capitalism*. 2d ed. New York: Basic Books.

Bermingham, Anne, and John Brewer, eds. 1996. *The Consumption of Culture, 1600–1800*. New York: Routledge.

Berry, John. 1994. *The Idea of Luxury: A Conceptual and Historical Investigation*. Cambridge: Cambridge University Press.

Black, Jeremy. 1990a. *British Politics from Walpole to Pitt, 1741–1789*. New York: St. Martin's Press.

———. 1990b. *Robert Walpole and the Nature of Politics in Early Eighteenth-Century Britain*. New York: St. Martin's Press.

———. 1984. *Britain in the Age of Walpole*. New York: St. Martin's Press.

Blackwell, Ron, Jaspal Chatha, and Edward Nell, eds. 1993. *Economics as a Worldly Philosophy: Essays in Political and Historical Economics in Honour of Robert L. Heilbroner*. New York: St. Martin's Press, 1993.

Block, Fred. 1991. "Contradictions of Self-Regulating Markets." In *The Legacy of Karl Polanyi*, ed. Marguerite Mendell and Daniel Salee. New York: St. Martin's Press.

———. 1987. *Revising State Theory: Essays in Politics and Post-Industrialism*. Philadelphia: Temple University Press.

Bok, Derek. 1995. *The State of the Nation: Government and the Quest for a Better Society*. Cambridge, Mass.: Harvard University Press.

Bolingbroke, Henry St. John, Viscount Bolingbroke. 1982. *Contributions to the Craftsman*, ed. Simon Varey. Oxford: Clarendon Press.

———. 1972. *Lord Bolingbroke: Historical Writings*, ed. Isaac Kramnick. Chicago: University of Chicago Press.

———. 1967. *The Works of Lord Bolingbroke*. 4 vols. London: Frank Cass and Company Limited.

Brewer, John, and John Styles, eds. 1980. *An Ungovernable People: The English and Their Law in the Seventeenth and Eighteenth Centuries*. New Brunswick: Rutgers University Press.

Brewer, John, and Roy Porter, eds. 1993. *Consumption and the World of Goods*. New York: Routledge.

Brewer, John, and Susan Staves, eds. 1995. *Early Modern Conceptions of Property*. New York: Routledge.

Brown, Vivienne. 1994. *Adam Smith's Discourse: Canonicity, Commerce, and Conscience*. London: Routledge.

Browning, Reed. 1982. *The Political and Constitutional Ideas of the Court Whigs*. Baton Rouge: Louisiana State University Press.

Bryner, Gary. 1987. *In Search of the Republic: Public Virtue and the Roots of American Government*. Totowa, N.J.: Rowman and Littlefield.

Burke, Edmund. 1854. *The Works of Edmund Burke, With a Memoir*. 2 vols. New York: Harper and Brothers.

Burtt, Shelley. 1992. *Virtue Transformed: Political Argument in England, 1688–1740*. Cambridge: Cambridge University Press.

Cannadine, David. 1994. *Aspects of Aristocracy: Grandeur and Decline in Modern Britain*. New Haven: Yale University Press.

———. 1990. *The Decline and Fall of the British Aristocracy*. New Haven: Yale University Press.

Cannon, John. 1984. *Aristocratic Century*. Cambridge: Cambridge University Press.

———, ed. 1981. *The Whig Ascendancy: Colloquies on Hanoverian England*. London: Edward Arnold.

Carswell, John. 1960. *The South Sea Bubble*. Stanford: Stanford University Press.

Clark, J. C. D. 1986. *Revolution and Rebellion: State and Society in England During the Seventeenth and Eighteenth Centuries*. Cambridge: Cambridge University Press.

Cockburn, J. S., ed. 1977. *Crime in England, 1500–1800*. Cambridge: Cambridge University Press.

Colker, Ruth. 1998. *American Law in the Age of Hypercapitalism: The Worker, the Family, and the State*. New York: New York University Press.

Colley, Linda. 1992. *Britons: Forging the Nation, 1707–1837*. New Haven: Yale University Press.

———. 1982. *In Defiance of Oligarchy: The Tory Party, 1714–60*. Cambridge: Cambridge University Press.

Cropsey, Joseph. 1957. *Polity and Economy: An Interpretation of the Principles of Adam Smith*. The Hague: Nijhoff.

Danziger, Sheldon, and Peter Gottschalk, eds. 1993. *Uneven Tides: Rising Inequality in America*. New York: Russell Sage Foundation.

Davidson, Lee, Tim Hitchcock, Tim Keirn, and Robert Shoemaker, eds. 1992. *Stilling the Grumbling Hive: The Response to Social and Economic Problems in England, 1689–1870*. New York: St. Martin's Press.

Defoe, Daniel. 1987. *Roxana, The Fortunate Mistress* (1724), ed. David Blewett. Harmondsworth: Penguin Books.

———. 1982. "A True and Genuine Account of the Life and Actions of the Late Jonathan Wild" (1725). In Henry Fielding, *The Life of Mr. Jonathan Wild, the Great*, ed. David Nokes, 229–56. Harmondsworth: Penguin Classics.

———. 1978. *Moll Flanders* (1722), ed. Juliet Mitchell. Harmondsworth: Penguin Books.

———. 1965. *Daniel Defoe*, ed. J. T. Boulton. New York: Schocken Books.

de Montalembert, Charles. 1969. "A Gentlemanly Rule—Not A Bureaucratic System." In *The English Ruling Class*, ed. W. L. Guttsman. London: Weidenfeld and Nicholson.

Dickey, Laurence. 1995. "Power, Commerce, and Natural Law in Daniel Defoe's Political Writings, 1698–1707." In *A Union for Empire: Political Thought and the British Union of 1707*, ed. John Robertson. Cambridge: Cambridge University Press.

———. 1993. "*Deux-Commerce* and the 'Mediocrity of Money' Problem" in *Adam Smith, An Inquiry into the Nature and Causes of the Wealth of Nations*, abridged, with commentary and notes by Laurence Dickey. Indianapolis: Hackett Publishing Company.

———. 1986. "Historicizing the Adam Smith Problem: Conceptual, Historiographical, and Textual Issues." *Journal of Modern History* 58, no. 3: 579–609.

Dickinson, H. T. 1977. *Liberty and Property: Political Ideology in Eighteenth-Century Britain*. London: Weidenfeld and Nicholson.

———. 1973. *Walpole and the Whig Supremacy*. London: English Universities Press.

Dunn, John. 1996. *The History of Political Theory and Other Essays*. Cambridge: Cambridge University Press.

———, ed. 1990. *The Economic Limits to Modern Politics*. Cambridge: Cambridge University Press.

———. 1985. *Rethinking Modern Political Theory*. Cambridge: Cambridge University Press.

Earle, Peter. 1989. *The Making of the English Middle Class: Business, Society, and Family Life in London, 1660–1730*. Berkeley and Los Angeles: University of California Press.

Ehrenreich, Barbara. 1990. *Fear of Falling: The Inner Life of the Middle Class*. New York: HarperCollins.

Esping-Andersen, Gosta, ed. 1996. *Welfare States in Transition: National Adaptations in Global Economies*. London: Sage Publications.

Farley, Reynolds. 1996. *The New American Reality.* New York: Russell Sage Foundation.

Ferguson, Adam. 1966. *An Essay on the History of Civil Society,* ed. Duncan Forbes. Edinburgh: Edinburgh University Press.

Fielding, Henry. 1989. *New Essays by Henry Fielding: His Contributions to the Craftsman 1734–1739 and Other Early Journalism,* ed. Michael G. Farringdon. Charlottesville: University Press of Virginia.

———. 1988. *An Inquiry into the Causes of the Late Increase of Robbers and Related Writings,* ed. Malvin R. Zirker. Middletown, Conn.: Wesleyan University Press.

———. 1987. *The True Patriot and Related Writings,* ed. W. B. Coley. Middletown, Conn.: Wesleyan University Press.

———. 1982. *The Life of Mr. Jonathan Wild, the Great* (1743), ed. David Nokes. Harmondsworth: Penguin Classics, 1982.

Fitzgibbons, Athol. 1995. *Adam Smith's System of Liberty, Wealth, and Virtue: The Moral and Political Foundations of The Wealth of Nations.* Oxford: Clarendon Press.

Fletcher, Andrew. 1979. *Selected Writings and Speeches,* ed. David Daisches. Edinburgh: Edinburgh University Press.

Forbes, Duncan. 1978. *Hume's Philosophical Politics.* Cambridge: Cambridge University Press.

———. 1975. "Skeptical Whiggism, Commerce, and Liberty." In *Essays on Adam Smith,* ed. Andrew S. Skinner and Thomas Wilson. Oxford: Clarendon Press.

Fox-Strangeways, Giles Stephen Holland, Earl of Illchester. 1950. *Lord John Hervey and His Friends.* London: John Murray.

Gay, John. *The Beggar's Opera* (1728), ed. Bryan Loughrey and T. O. Treadwell. Harmondsworth: Penguin Classics.

Gee, James, Glynda Hull, and Colin Lankshear. 1996. *The New Work Order: Behind the Language of the New Capitalism.* Boulder: Westview Press.

Gerson, Mark, ed. 1996. *The Essential Neoconservative Reader.* New York: Addison-Wesley Publishing Company.

Gilder, George. 1981. *Wealth and Poverty.* New York: Basic Books.

Girouard, Mark. 1978. *Life in the English Country House: A Social and Architectural History.* New Haven: Yale University Press.

Goldgar, Bertrand A. 1976. *Walpole and the Wits: The Relation of Politics to Literature, 1722–1742.* University of Nebraska Press.

Goldsmith, M. M. 1988. "Regulating Anew the Moral and Political Sentiments of Mankind: Bernard Mandeville and the Scottish Enlightenment." *Journal of the History of Ideas* 49 (October–December): 587–606.

———. 1985. *Private Vices and Public Benefits: Bernard Mandeville's Social and Political Thought.* Cambridge: Cambridge University Press.

Gordon, Thomas Gordon, and John Trenchard. 1969. *Cato's Letters.* New York: Russell and Russell.

Groenewegen, Peter, ed. 1996. *Economics and Ethics?* London and New York: Routledge.

Gunn, J. A. W. 1983. *Beyond Liberty and Property: The Process of Self-Recognition in Eighteenth-Century Political Thought*. Kingston, Ont.: McGill-Queen's University Press.

———. 1969. *Politics and the Public Interest in the Seventeenth Century*. London: Routledge and Kegan Paul.

Handler, Joel F., and Yeheskel Hasenfeld. 1997. *We the Poor People: Work, Poverty, and Welfare*. New Haven: Yale University Press.

Harte, Negley Roland Quinault, ed. 1996. *Land and Society in Britain, 1700–1914: Essays in Honour of F. M. L. Thompson*. Manchester: Manchester University Press.

Hay, Douglas, ed. 1975. *Albion's Fatal Tree: Crime and Society in Eighteenth-Century England*. London: A. Lane Publishers.

Hayek, F. A. 1978. *Studies in Philosophy, Politics, Economics, and the History of Ideas*. Chicago: University of Chicago Press.

———. 1944. *The Road to Serfdom*. New York: Routledge and Kegan Paul.

Heilbroner, Robert L. 1988. *Behind the Veil of Economics: Essays in the Worldly Philosophy*. New York: Norton and Company.

———. 1982. "The Socialization of the Individual in Adam Smith." *History of Political Economy* 14, no. 3: 421–31.

———. 1975. "The Paradox of Progress: Decline and Decay in the *Wealth of Nations*." In *Essays on Adam Smith*, ed. Andrew S. Skinner and Thomas Wilson. Oxford: Clarendon Press.

Hemingway, Andrew. 1989. "The 'Sociology' of Taste in the Scottish Enlightenment." *Oxford Art Journal* 12, no. 2: 3–35.

Henry Horowitz. 1992. "Liberty, Law, and Property, 1689–1776." In *Liberty Secured?: Britain Before and After 1688*, ed. J. R. Jones. Stanford: Stanford University Press.

Herman, Edward S. 1995. *Triumph of the Market: Essays on Economics, Politics, and the Media*. Boston: South End Press.

Herrnstein, Richard J., and Charles Murray. 1994. *The Bell Curve: Intelligence and Class Structure in American Life*. New York: The Free Press.

Hervey, John, Lord Hervey. 1985. *Ancient and Modern Liberty Stated and Compar'd*. (1734), ed. H. T. Dickinson. Los Angeles: William Clark Memorial Library.

Herzog, Don. 1986. "Some Questions for Republicans." *Political Theory* 14, no. 3: 473–93.

Himmelfarb, Gertrude. 1995. *The De-Moralization of Society: From Victorian Virtues to Modern Values*. New York: Alfred A. Knopf.

Hirschman, Albert O. 1986. *Rival Views of Market Society and Other Recent Essays*. New York: Viking Penguin.

———. 1977. *The Passions and the Interests: Political Arguments for Capitalism Before Its Triumph*. Princeton: Princeton University Press.

Holmes, G. S., 1982. *Augustan England: Professions, State, and Society, 1680–1730*. London: George Allen and Unwin.

Holmes, G. S., and W. A. Speck, eds. 1967. *The Divided Society: Party and Politics in England 1694–1716*. New York: St. Martin's Press.

Hont, Istvan Michael Ignatieff, eds. 1983. *Wealth and Virtue: The Shaping of Political Economy in the Scottish Enlightenment*. Cambridge: Cambridge University Press.

Horne, Thomas. 1978. *The Social Thought of Bernard Mandeville*. New York: Columbia University Press.

Hume, David. 1987. *Essays Moral, Political, and Literary*, ed. Eugene Miller. Indianapolis: Liberty Classics.

———. 1957. *An Inquiry into the Principles of Morals*, ed. Charles W. Hendel. Indianapolis: Bobbs-Merrill.

———. 1948. *Hume's Moral and Political Philosophy*, ed. Henry D. Aiken. New York: Hafner Publishing Company.

Hundert, E. G. 1994. *The Enlightenment's Fable: Bernard Mandeville and the Discovery of Society*. Cambridge: Cambridge University Press.

Plumb J. H. 1967. *The Origins of Political Stability: England, 1675–1725*. Boston: Houghton Mifflin.

Jones, J. R. *Liberty Secured?: Britain Before and After 1688*. Stanford: Stanford University Press.

Jones, Peter, and Andrew Skinner, eds. 1992. *Adam Smith Reviewed*. Edinburgh: Edinburgh University Press.

Kozodoy, Neal, ed. 1995. *What to Do About . . . A Collection of Essays from* Commentary Magazine. New York: Regan Books.

Kramnick, Isaac. 1968. *Bolingbroke and His Circle: The Politics of Nostalgia in the Age of Walpole*. Cambridge, Mass.: Harvard University Press.

Kuttner, Robert. 1997. *Everything for Sale: The Virtues and Limits of Markets*. New York: Alfred A. Knopf.

Langford, Paul. 1986. *Walpole and the Robinocracy: The English Saterical Print, 1600–1832*. Cambridge: Chadwick-Healey.

Laslett, Peter. 1965. *The World We Have Lost: England Before the Industrial Age*. New York: Charles Scribner's Sons.

———. 1965. *The World We Have Lost: Further Explored*. New York: Charles Scribner's Sons.

Linebaugh, Peter. 1992. *The London Hanged: Crime and Civil Society in the Eighteenth Century*. Cambridge: Cambridge University Press.

Mackay, Charles. 1841. *Memoirs of Extraordinary Popular Delusions and the Madness of Crowds*. London: Richard Bentley.

MacPherson, C. B., ed. 1978. *Property: Mainstream and Critical Positions*. Toronto: University of Toronto Press.

Madrick, Jeffrey. 1995. *The End of Affluence: The Causes and Consequences of America's Economic Decline*. New York: Random House.

Malthus, Thomas. *An Essay on the Principle of Population*, ed. Donald Winch. Cambridge: Cambridge University Press.

Mandeville, Bernard. 1976. *A Treatise of the Hypocrondriak and Hysterick Passions; vulgarly call'd the Hypo in Men and the Vapours in Women* (1711), ed. Stephen H. Good. Delmar, N.Y.: Scholars' Facsimiles and Reprints.

————. 1966. *The Fable of the Bees* (1723), ed. F. B. Kaye. 2 vols. Oxford: Oxford University Press.

————. 1964. *An Inquiry into the frequent Executions at Tyburn; and a Proposal for some Regulations concerning Felons in Prison, and the Good Effects to be expected from them* (1725), ed. Malvin R. Zirker. Los Angeles: Augustan Reprint Society.

Matthews, Richard K., ed. 1994. *Virtue, Corruption, and Self-Interest: Political Values in the Eighteenth Century*. Bethlehem: Lehigh University Press.

McKendrick, Neil, ed. 1974. *Historical Perspectives: Studies in English Thought and Society in Honour of J. H. Plumb*. London: Europa Publishers.

McNally, David. 1988. *Political Economy and the Rise of Capitalism*. Berkeley and Los Angeles: University of California Press.

Meek, Ronald. 1977. *Smith, Marx, and After: Ten Essays in the Development of Economic Thought*. New York: Wiley and Sons.

Meir, Thomas Keith. 1987. *Defoe and the Defense of Commerce*. Victoria, B.C.: English Literary Studies, University of Victoria.

Millar, John. 1960. *John Millar of Glasgow*, ed. W. C. Lehmann. Cambridge: Cambridge University Press.

Miller, David. 1981. *Philosophy and Ideology in Hume's Political Thought*. Oxford: Clarendon Press.

Mills, Nicolaus. 1997. *The Triumph of Meanness: America's War Against Its Better Self*. New York: Houghton Mifflin Company.

Minowitz, Peter. 1993. *Profits, Priests, and Princes: Adam Smith's Emancipation of Economics from Politics and Religion*. Stanford: Stanford University Press.

Monro, Hector. 1975. *The Ambivalence of Bernard Mandeville*. Oxford: Oxford University Press.

Morgan, Marjorie. 1994. *Manners, Morals, and Class in England, 1774–1858*. New York: St. Martin's Press.

Murray, Patrick, ed. 1997. *Reflections on Commercial Life: An Anthology of Classic Texts From Plato to the Present*. New York: Routledge.

Nelson, John S., ed. 1986. *Tradition, Interpretation, and Science: Political Theory in the American Academy*. Albany: State University of New York Press.

Pagden, Anthony, ed. 1987. *The Languages of Political Theory in Early Modern Europe*. Cambridge: Cambridge University Press.

Plumb, J. H. 1967. *The Origins of Political Stability in England, 1675–1725*. Boston: Houghton Mifflin Company.

Pocock, J. G. A. 1985. *Virtue, Commerce, and History: Essays on Political Thought and History, Chiefly in the Eighteenth Century*. Cambridge: Cambridge University Press.

————. 1981. "The Machiavellian Moment Revisited: A Study in History and Ideology." *Journal of Modern History* 53: 49–72.

————. 1976. "1776: The Revolution Against Parliament." In *Three British Revolutions*, ed. J. G. A. Pocock. Princeton: Princeton University Press.

————. 1975. *The Machiavellian Moment: Florentine Political Thought and the Atlantic Republican Tradition*. Princeton: Princeton University Press.

————. 1967. *The Ancient Constitution and the Feudal Law: English Historical Thought in the Seventeenth Century*. New York: W. W. Norton.

Pocock, J. G. A., Gordon Schochet, and Lois G. Schwoerer, eds. 1993. *The Varieties of British Political Thought, 1500–1800*. Cambridge: Cambridge University Press.

Polanyi, Karl. 1944. *The Great Transformation*. Boston: Beacon Press.

Pope, Alexander. 1991. *Pope's Dunciad of 1728: A History and Facsimile*, ed. David L. Vander Meulen. Charlottesville: University Press of Virginia.

Porter, Roy. 1992. "Georgian Britain: An Ancien Regime?" *British Journal of Eighteenth-Century Studies* 15: 141–44.

Primer, Irwin, ed. 1975. *Mandeville Studies: New Explorations in the Art and Thought of Dr. Bernard Mandeville*. The Hague: Martinus Nijhoff.

Rogers, Daniel T. 1992. "Republicanism: The Career of a Concept." *Journal of Modern History* 79 (June 1992): 11–38.

Rossiter, Clinton, ed. 1961. *The Federalist Papers*. New York: New American Library.

Rubenstein, W. D. 1996. "Businessmen into Landowners: The Question Revisited." In *Land and Society in Britain, 1700–1914: Essays in Honour of F. M. L. Thompson*, ed. Negley Harte and Roland Quinault. Manchester: Manchester University Press.

Rubini, Dennis. 1967. *Court and Country, 1688–1702*. London: Rupert Hart-Davis.

Ryan, Allen. 1984. *Property and Political Theory*. Oxford: Blackwell.

Sandel, Michael. 1985. "The State and the Soul." *New Republic*, 39–42.

Schonhorn, Manuel. 1991. *Defoe's Politics: Parliament, Power, Kingship, and Robinson Crusoe*. Cambridge: Cambridge University Press.

Shapiro, Ian. 1990. "Pocock's Republicanism." *Critical Review* 4, no. 3 (summer): 433–63.

Shapiro, Michael J. 1993. *Reading "Adam Smith": Desire, History, and Value*. New York: Sage Publications.

Skinner, Andrew, and Thomas Wilson, eds. 1976. *Essays on Adam Smith*. Oxford: Oxford University Press.

Smith, Adam. 1982. *Essays on Philosophical Subjects*, ed. W. P. D. Wightman and J. C. Bryce. Indianapolis: Liberty Classics.

————. 1976. *An Inquiry into the Nature and Causes of the Wealth of Nations* (1776), ed. R. H. Campbell and A. S. Skinner. 2 vols. Indianapolis: Liberty Classics.

————. 1976. *The Theory of Moral Sentiments*, ed. D. D. Raphael and A. L. Macfie. Indianapolis: Liberty Classics.

Solkin, David H. 1993. *Painting for Money: The Visual Arts and the Public Sphere in Eighteenth-Century England*. New Haven: Yale University Press.

Speck, W. A. 1977. *Stability and Strife: England, 1714–1760*. Cambridge, Mass.: Harvard University Press.

Stefanic, Jean, and Richard Delgado. 1996. *No Mercy: How Conservative Think Tanks and Foundations Changed America's Social Agenda*. Philadelphia: Temple University Press.

Thompson, E. P. 1991. *Customs in Common*. London: The Merlin Press,

———. 1975. *Whigs and Hunters: The Origin of the Black Act*. New York: Pantheon Books.

Paine, Tom. 1987. *The Thomas Paine Reader*, ed. Michael Foote and Isaac Kramnick. New York: Viking Penguin.

Tully, James, and Quentin Skinner, eds. 1988. *Meaning and Context: Quentin Skinner and His Critics*. Princeton: Princeton University Press.

Turner, Michael, ed. 1986. *Malthus and His Time*. New York: St. Martin's Press.

Viner, Jacob. 1991. *Essays on the Intellectual History of Economics*. Princeton: Princeton University Press.

Walton, John, and David Seddon, ed. 1994. *Free Markets and Food Riots: The Politics of Global Adjustment*. Cambridge, Mass.: Blackwell Publishers.

Winch, Donald. 1996. *Riches and Poverty: An Intellectual History of Political Economy in Britain, 1750–1834*. Cambridge: Cambridge University Press.

———. 1978. *Adam Smith's Politic: An Essay in Historiographic Revision*. Cambridge: Cambridge University Press.

Wolff, Edward N. 1995. *Top Heavy: A Study of the Increasing Inequality of Wealth in America*. New York: The Twentieth Century Fund.

Wolin, Sheldon. 1989. *The Presence of the Past: Essays on the State and the Constitution*. Baltimore: Johns Hopkins University Press.

———. 1960. *Politics and Vision*. Boston: Little Brown.

Wollstonecraft, Mary. 1977. *A Wollstonecraft Anthology*, ed. Janet M. Todd. Bloomington: Indiana University Press.

Wood, Gordon. 1992. *The Radicalism of the American Revolution* New York: Alfred A. Knopf.

———. 1969. *The Creation of the American Republic*. Chapel Hill: University of North Carolina Press.

Wooten, David, ed. 1994. *Republicanism, Liberty, and Commercial Society, 1649–1776*. Stanford: Stanford University Press.

Index

Phillipson, Nicholas, 7, 113n.19
Pocock, J. G. A., 6–7, 11–12, 109n.6; on republicanism, 11–12, 113n.22
Polanyi, Karl, 109n.2
political theory: free enterprise and political
incompetence, 91–99; history of, 115n.31;
Hume on authority in commercial society,
62–67; Hume's primacy of passion and,
55–62; Mandeville's development of, 21–23;
moral corruption and political economy,
25–28; paradigms of, 5–6, 108–9n.2; role of
aristocracy in, 3; Smith on insignificance of
political power, 97–99; Smith's contribution to, 6, 69–70, 78–82, 101–5, 121n.1;
Smith's moral philosophy and political
economy, 82–86
Pope, Alexander, 9, 30
popular culture, role of aristocracy in, 1–3
population theory, 103–5
Porter, Cole, 47
poverty: Fielding's work on, 121n.10; Mandeville's economic theory and, 26–28; Smith
on happiness and, 80–82; Smith on social
rejection of, 74–76
"Power of the Prince," 38
"primitive purity," Bolingbroke's concept of,
38–39
private interest. See free enterprise; individualism; self-interest
prodigality: Mandeville's views on, 19–20,
116n.9; Smith's views on political consequences of, 93–95. See also frugality
property: authority and, 65–67; class structure and, 1–2; commerce and transformation of, 62–67; Hume on rights and
obligations and, 55–62; Mandeville's political theories and, 30–33; political economy
and, 11; political power and, 60–62;
Smith's theories on competition and property ownership, 93–99, 124n.35; social evolution and ownership of, 85
public credit. See national debt

Rae, John, 77
Reagan, Ronald, 113n.22
Reform Act of 1832, 3
republicanism: Bolingbroke on political de-
spair and, 44–48; commercial ideology
and, 6–7, 11–12; historical relevance of, 14;
Smith's political theory and, 70–71
Revolution Settlement of 1688, 36

riches. See luxury; property; wealth
Robertson, John, 7, 113n.19

scientific theory, Smith's observations on,
122n.14
Scottish political economy, 10–13
"Search into the Nature of Society, A," 20
self-interest: Hume on justice and, 55–62;
oblivion and pursuit of, 86–90; Smith on
morality and, 72, 84–85
Shaftesbury, third earl of, 20
Shapiro, Ian, 113n.22
"skilful Politician," Mandeville's concept of,
22–23, 116n.11
Skinner, Quentin, 118n.13
Smith, Adam, 1; American Constitution and,
54; aristocracy examined by, 3–7, 13, 47–
48, 66–67, 69–99; Bolingbroke's theories
and, 47–48; "civic moralist" view of,
113n.19; commerce and political theories of,
5–8; County party ideology and, 10,
112n.17; on division of labor, 113n.31; on
human happiness, 76–82; Hume and, 54;
Marx's critique of, 121n.1; morality and political reform, 10–11, 13–14, 69–99; moral
philosophy and transition to political economy, 82–85, 122n.14; political incompetence and free enterprise and, 91–99;
political theory of, 86–91, 123n.24; on unreality of social elites, 72–76
social contract theory: Hume's view of, 57–59;
Mandeville's view of, 21
social development: Smith on politics and,
70–72
social elite. See aristocracy; class structure
social hierarchy (social stratification). See class
structure
social relations, Mandeville's view of, 21, 56
South Sea Bubble, 16–17, 43
sovereigns, Smith's view of, 95–99
"Spirit of Patriotism," 78–79
stock trading: Bolingbroke on consequences
of, 42–44, 46–48; Hume on national debt
and, 52–54
Swift, Jonathan, 9

Theory of Moral Sentiments, 13, 32, 65, 70–71,
119n.12; human happiness described in,
76–82; moral philosophy and political
economy in, 18, 83–85, 122n.14; unreality of
social elite in, 72–76